DELEGATED
LEGISLATION

DELEGATED LEGISLATION

THREE LECTURES

BY

CECIL T. CARR, LL.D.

OF THE INNER TEMPLE, BARRISTER-AT-LAW

CAMBRIDGE

AT THE UNIVERSITY PRESS

1921

CAMBRIDGE
UNIVERSITY PRESS

University Printing House, Cambridge CB2 8BS, United Kingdom

Cambridge University Press is part of the University of Cambridge.

It furthers the University's mission by disseminating knowledge in the pursuit of
education, learning and research at the highest international levels of excellence.

www.cambridge.org
Information on this title: www.cambridge.org/9781316606902

© Cambridge University Press 1921

First published 1921
First paperback edition 2016

A catalogue record for this publication is available from the British Library

ISBN 978-1-316-60690-2 Paperback

PREFACE

THIS book contains the substance of three lectures on "Delegated Legislation" delivered at Cambridge in April, 1921, with the sanction of the Law Board.

The title was suggested by Sir Courtenay Ilbert, who in his classic "Legislative Methods and Forms," published twenty years ago and now out of print, described this field of law-making as an important region as yet imperfectly explored. The significance of the Statutory Rule and Order system had not escaped Maitland when in 1888 he composed the notes which afterwards formed his volume on Constitutional Law. To these two teachers the student must resort for a general view in correct perspective, but the subject is important enough to deserve a more particular and frequent treatment. The recent organisation of the realm for its successful defence favoured departmental expansion and multiplied regulations—a process from which reaction, though visible, is slow. Perhaps, therefore, the moment may not be thought inopportune for drawing attention to a branch of law which so closely touches the form of the statute book, the liberty of the subject, the supremacy of Parliament, and the administration of the country. With the offensives and counter-offensives of party politics the following pages have no concern. The zeal of either party in attacking the other for encouraging the encroachments of officialism is—as Sir Frederick Pollock has said—naturally tempered by the reflection that the accusing party has itself made statutes of that kind by the score, and will want to make them again when it comes back to office. Yet, when these controversies have been thus discounted, there remain big issues for the plain citizen. If it is he who has to suffer, it is he who has the remedy.

The first lecture (represented by Chapters I and II of the present book) was designed to show how much our laws as nowadays made by Parliament depend for their understanding and their working upon laws to be subsequently made by somebody else. The second lecture (Chapters III and IV) attempts to explain how administrative convenience and national necessity have brought this situation about, and how far our liberties, if thereby imperilled, can be protected by safeguards. The third lecture (Chapters V and VI) deals with the form and publication of Statutory Rules and Orders and concludes with some observations on the historical development by which delegated legislation has replaced prerogative legislation. A few short Statutory Rules and Orders are, with the permission of the Controller of H.M. Stationery Office, printed as illustrations in an Appendix. The Rules Publication Act of 1893 and the Treasury Regulations made thereunder in 1894 are added for convenient reference.

These chapters do not pretend to be exhaustive. When Mr Alexander Pulling, the learned editor of so many annual volumes of Statutory Rules and Orders and so many manuals of emergency legislation, is persuaded to give us the fruits of his unique experience, the task will be in the proper hands. His prefaces to the original "Annual Volume of Statutory Rules and Orders" (issued in 1890) and to the original "Index to Statutory Rules and Orders" (issued in 1891) first revealed the need of an orderly system of collecting and publishing the already considerable output of subsidiary or departmental law-making. When in 1893 Parliament laid down the lines along which such publication should continue, his Annual Volumes for the past years (from 1890 to 1892) were officially prescribed as the model for the future. Mr Pulling's qualifications to be the historian and expounder of delegated legislation need no further advertisement. His generous approval of the idea of delivering the lectures whereof the present book has been the outcome is one of many kindnesses for which the apprentice is grateful to the master.

It is a pleasant duty to thank friends at Cambridge for their encouragement, especially Professor Hazeltine, Mr Henry Hollond and Mr Arthur Goodhart.

C. T. C.

July 20, 1921

CONTENTS

CHAPTER I

INTRODUCTORY

BENTHAM'S "General View of a Complete Code of Laws" daily grows dimmer. He wanted the citizen to have easy access to an orderly and intelligible digest free from the need of professional interpretation on the part of the fee-collecting fraternity. "Citizen," the legislator was to say, "what is your condition? Are you a father? Open the chapter 'Of Fathers.' Are you an agriculturist? Open the chapter 'Of Agriculture[1].'"

For better or for worse the ideal remains unrealised. We are not in a position to give such simple directions to inquirers. When we offer the citizen-father the Acts about education we have to add that he will not understand how they work unless he also studies the codes and regulations issued thereunder by the Board of Education. When we offer the citizen-farmer the Acts about agriculture, we have also to draw his attention to a multitude of leaflets containing departmental instructions about adulteration of milk, diseases of animals, corn production (for the present year at any rate), destruction of insects and pests, drainage of land, maintenance of live-stock, weighing of cattle, tithes, and the wages of agricultural labourers.

Everywhere in our statute book the same process is visible. The action of our Acts of Parliament grows more and more dependent upon subsidiary legislation. More than half our modern Acts are to this extent incomplete statements of law. If anyone opens at random a recent annual volume of public general statutes, he will not have to turn many pages before finding a provision that His Majesty may make Orders in Council, or that some public body or officer or department may make rules or regulations, contributing some addition to the substance or the detail or the working of that particular Act. When the King in Parliament, our supreme law-making authority, expressly allows some other authority to undertake this kind of

[1] Bentham, "Works" (ed. Bowring), iii, p. 193.

supplementary law-making, the result is what we call "delegated legislation[1]."

Blackstone gave currency to the artificial division of English law into *lex scripta* and *lex non scripta*. With the latter we are not now concerned. The former—the written law—has been again divided into three parts. The first and now far the smallest part is made by the Crown under what survives of the prerogative. The second and weightiest part is made by the King in Parliament and consists of what we call Acts of Parliament. The third and bulkiest part is made by such persons or bodies as the King in Parliament entrusts with legislative power. It is with this last part that these pages will deal. It is directly related to Acts of Parliament, related as child to parent, a growing child called upon to relieve the parent of the strain of overwork and capable of attending to minor matters while the parent manages the main business.

In mere bulk the child now dwarfs the parent. Last year, while 82 Acts of Parliament were placed on the statute book, more than ten times as many "Statutory Rules and Orders[1]" of a public character were officially registered under the Rules Publication Act. The annual volume of public general statutes for 1920 occupied less than 600 pages; the two volumes of statutory rules and orders for the same period occupy about five times as many. This excess in mere point of bulk of delegated legislation over direct legislation has been visible for nearly thirty years.

To anyone who is studying the general principles of law rather than any special subject of law, these statistics need cause no alarm. It is enough that he should know of the existence of this large field of subsidiary or supplementary legislation and that he should know how to find his way to it and about it if he so desires. With the ordinary citizen, on the other hand, it is different. He is not particularly interested in general principles; the supplementary departmental legislation may be just what he most wants to know. When must he alter his breakfast-

---

[1] When officially published under the Rules Publication Act, delegated legislation is called "Statutory Rules and Orders"; but not all delegated legislation is so published. See p. 45, below. The total of Rules and Orders officially registered for 1920 was 2473.

room clock or his wrist-watch for summer-time? It is not an Act but an Order in Council which tells him[1]. What interest can he get on a Housing Bond? The Housing Acts leave that point to be fixed by the Treasury. How does he register his motor-car and on what part of the car must he display the licence and the identification marks? The Roads Act is silent, or merely refers him to regulations to be made by the Minister of Transport. What is the official date of the legal end of the war? The Act tells him to look out for Orders in Council. How much postage will be charged on a $3\frac{1}{2}$-ounce letter to Cambridge, or a parcel of newspapers to Paris or India? All that the Post Office Acts say is that the Treasury may fix these charges on the representation of the Postmaster-General. Of course one can inquire at the Post Office during working hours, or one can study the Postal Guide if the copy is not out of date; but the point is that one will not find the information in a statute but somewhere else because Parliament has realised the convenience of delegating the legislation about these matters. As for summer-time and the end of the war and so on, the morning paper will doubtless tell us if anything startling happens. But we have not yet accepted Government by press *communiqué*, nor are we yet schooled to believe all that we read. Are we legally obliged to read the newspaper?

We have an odious half-truth that "everybody is supposed to know the law." It pricks our conscience as citizens. "Lord!" wrote Pepys in his diary, "what a shame methinks to me that in this condition and at this age I should know no better the laws of my own country." Is there not a legal as well as a moral obligation? "All the King's subjects," says a modern authority, "must be taken to know the statute law[2]." If a conscientious citizen asks whether it is his duty to study not only all the statutes but the delegated legislation as well, we cannot answer him without a little digression.

The Digest did indeed declare that nobody is excused by ignorance of law—*ignorantia juris quod quisque scire tenetur*, the

---

[1] See the Order printed as an illustration at p. 66 below.
[2] Halsbury, "Laws of England," vol. xxvii, p. 114. S. 28 (1) of the Unemployment Insurance Act, 1920, seems to expect that the Act will be misunderstood. Enactments "to remove doubts" are not unknown.

law which everyone is held to know[1]. If we had lived in Rome in those days and had had to do as the Romans did, we should have found some little mitigation. There were certain occasionally fortunate persons *quibus permissum est jus ignorare*—soldiers *propter imperitiam*, women *propter sexus infirmitatem*, young persons under the age of twenty-five with no lawyer to advise them. Nobody can plead those mitigations in England to-day when hundreds of lawyers have lately been soldiers, hundreds of ladies are going to be lawyers and hundreds of young persons are maliciously said to be as near omniscience before the age of twenty-five as at any time afterwards. We have no classes of persons *quibus permissum est jus ignorare*. All we can do is to treasure certain comfortable sayings. Lord Westbury of blessed memory has said that the common man need not know the equitable doctrine of election[2]. Lord Mansfield declared that if the law was so certain that everybody knew it, it would be very hard on the profession[3]. Mr Justice Maule laboured to prove the existence of doubtful points of law and pertinently inquired whether the existence of Courts of Appeal did not indicate that even judges might be afflicted with *ignorantia juris*. Indeed Mr Justice Maule's remarks in *Martindale* v. *Falkner*[4] are the best summary of the position:

There is no presumption in this country that every person knows the law. It would be contrary to common sense and reason if it were so. The rule is ignorance of the law shall not excuse a man or relieve him from the consequences of crime, or from liability upon a contract.

Perhaps the statement that "All the King's subjects must be taken to know the statute law" is chiefly based on the principle that our Acts of Parliament ordinarily take effect without previous warning or promulgation. But here again there are judicial dicta which contain some comfort. Particular persons, it seems, must know particular laws; by implication we dare hope that other persons need not. An insurance agent, it is said,

---

[1] See Digest, 22, 6.
[2] In *Spread* v. *Morgan* (1864) 11 H.L.C. 602.
[3] In *Jones* v. *Randall* (1774) Cowp. at p. 42.
[4] (1846) 2 C.B. at p. 719: 66 R.R. at p. 611. See the complete statement of the law in Pollock on Contracts, chap. IX.

should at any rate know insurance law[1]. Candidates for municipal office should be familiar with the law of municipal elections[2]. Most striking of all "it is not the duty of a solicitor"—a solicitor who pledges his skill and takes our money for it—"it is not the duty of a solicitor to know the contents of every statute of the realm[3]" though he really ought to know the Public Authorities Protection Act of 1893. Does it not look as though, if we never intend to have anything to do with insurance or to sue a public authority, we might safely ignore the law on those subjects? If a man has no income, *cantabit vacuus*, can he not whistle in the face of the 180 pages of the Income Tax Act of 1918 and its subsequent amendments? After all, need we take the maxim more seriously than Maitland did who found in it the explanation of the honorary degrees in law given by universities to potentates and politicians? "Impossible to convict them of divinity or medicine, it was convenient to fall back on the legal principle that everyone must be taken to know the law sufficiently well to be a doctor thereof[4]."

To end the digression we can say that, whether legal truth or legal fiction, the maxim represents a rule of overwhelming convenience. Judges are busy enough saying what the law is, without having to decide what litigants think it is. As for the duty to know delegated legislation, it must be the same as the duty to know the Acts of Parliament which give birth to it and to which it is complementary. Bye-laws are as good law as Acts of Parliament, except that an Act cannot be judicially questioned whereas delegated legislation can[5], though the odds are against the questioner. Sometimes Parliament expressly says that the delegated legislation shall have just as much force as the Act which authorises it. The exact meaning of such a provision has

---

[1] Per Alverstone L.C.J., *Harse* v. *Pearl Life Assurance Co.* [1903] 2 K.B. (reversed on appeal) at p. 97.

[2] Per Rowlatt J., *In re Municipal Corporations Act,* 1874, *etc. ex parte Groom,* "The Times" newspaper, Nov. 2, 1920.

[3] Per Scrutton L.J., *Fletcher & Son* v. *Jubb, Booth and Halliwell* [1920], 1 K.B. at p. 281.

[4] "Collected Papers," 1, p. 495.

[5] See Lord Herschell L.C., *Institute of Patent Agents* v. *Lockwood* [1894] A.C. at pp. 359–60, Lord Abinger, *Hopkins* v. *Mayor of Swansea,* 4 M. & W. at p. 640, and Holt C.J. in *City of London* v. *Wood,* 12 Mod. at p. 678.

been disputed[1], but we can close this introduction with a statement which is indisputable. The direct legislation of Parliament cannot be treated as something separate and self-contained; the statute book is not only incomplete but even misleading unless it be read with the delegated legislation which amplifies and amends it.

[1] See *Institute of Patent Agents* v. *Lockwood* [1894] A.C. 347. In *The King* v. *Inspector of Cannon-Row Police Station, ex parte Brady*, (1921) 37 T.L.R. at p. 856, Lawrence L.C.J. thought that it was not open to the Court to hold that a Regulation made under the Restoration of Order in Ireland Act was *ultra vires* since 10–1 G. 5, c. 31, s. 1 (4) provided that such regulations should "have effect as if enacted in this Act." For the right of judicial challenge, apparently jeopardised by the insertion of these words, see pp. 29–31 below.

CHAPTER II

EFFECT ON THE STATUTE BOOK

DELEGATED LEGISLATION is allowed to affect the statute book in three different ways which we will now examine. But, first of all, what is the statute book?

The statute book is a collection of all the Acts of Parliament in force. The earliest of them dates from 1235, and there are thus nearly seven centuries of what we now call Public General Acts wholly or partly unrepealed. In its least inconvenient form the collection consists of:

(a) twenty substantial volumes (revised at various dates but with further revision sadly in arrear) containing all Acts passed down to the end of Queen Victoria's reign;

(b) annual volumes from 1900 onwards; and

(c) single unbound copies of any Acts passed since the last annual volume was issued.

There is an officially published guide called a "Chronological Table and Index to the Statutes in Force" which tries to map out the strata which successive generations of law-makers have been depositing for these seven hundred years and to show how far any particular section of an Act has been repealed, amended or otherwise affected by subsequent Acts. There are few branches of law in which it will not be necessary for the practitioner to consult several of these volumes at once. As a collection our statute book might be summed up as beyond the average citizen's pocket to purchase, beyond his book-shelves to accommodate, beyond his leisure to study and beyond his intellect to comprehend.

However let us make the optimistic assumption that some capable and conscientious citizen has got access to a copy, has noted up against each section of each Act the repeals and substitutions and amendments made by later Acts, has mastered the principles of the much abused but partly inevitable practice of "legislation by reference," and in short has acquainted himself with all that the statute book can tell him. What are the three ways in which delegated legislation introduces further complications?

They are, firstly, direct amendment of an Act; secondly, the creation of some additional machinery affecting the commencement, duration or application of an Act; and, thirdly, the elaboration of detail—especially in matters of procedure or of minor importance—to facilitate the objects or working of an Act.

Instances of these three (which sometimes overlap one another) will serve to show the immense administrative value of the system.

A. DIRECT AMENDMENT

Here are a few haphazard examples of direct amendment of statute by statutory rules and orders. Anyone can soon find other examples and probably better ones.

The Companies Act of 1908 contained certain tables and forms in schedules, but it allowed the Board of Trade to vary those tables and to add to those forms (8 E. 7, c. 69, s. 118).

A schedule to the Metropolitan Police Act of 1839 contained a table of fees for taking out a summons or a warrant and so on. A later Act in 1897 provided that this table might be altered by the Home Office (60–1 V. c. 26, s. 2 (2)).

An Act of 1799 specified the rates of brokerage to be charged by Dublin stockbrokers on dealings in Government securities. In 1918 Parliament allowed the Lord Lieutenant to approve rules fixed by the Dublin Stock Exchange in substitution for those in the 1799 Act (8–9 G. 5, c. 46, s. 1).

The Weights and Measures Act of 1878 contained a table of metric equivalents. A later Act in 1897 sanctioned the varying of the table by Order in Council (60–1 V. c. 46, s. 2 (2)).

In 1882 it occurred to Parliament to protect ancient monuments such as Stonehenge and other similar relics of the past. For this purpose a number of Druid circles, earthworks, chapels, crosses, etc., were scheduled as "ancient monuments." Parliament at the same time permitted the Crown in Council to add other monuments to the original schedule (45–6 V. c. 73, s. 10; see 3–4 G. 5, c. 32, ss. 14 (4), 24, sch. 2).

Our last example in this series shows the legislative power entrusted in part to a professional organisation. Such delegation need occasion no remark in a country where gild-like organisations have supervised trade from time immemorial, and where the goodly fellowships of goldsmiths and gunmakers, scriveners and stationers and the like have hardly yet relinquished all their rights of control. An Act of 1868 contained a schedule of poisons and forbade unqualified persons to deal with such substances. But the Act allowed the schedule to be from time to time enlarged so as to include any fresh substance which the Pharmaceutical Society of Great Britain (with the approval of the Privy Council and after due advertisement in the "London Gazette") should declare to be a poison within the meaning of the Act (31–2 V. c. 121, s. 2; 8 E. 7, c. 55, s. 1, sch.).

Now this kind of legislative detail, which draftsmen usually relegate to the schedule of an Act of Parliament, is not like the laws of the Medes and Persians. Developments of scientific research (if it be a matter of poisons) or changes in the purchasing value of money (if it be a matter of fees) justify an elastic method. Why should Parliamentary time be occupied with the passing of a new Act merely because the doctors have come to the conclusion that ecgonine and heroin ought to be added to the statutory schedule of poisons? If a representative body of chemists is agreed, if the Privy Council consents and if we are all warned, let the matter be dealt with by delegated legislation. Matters mutable and fluctuating are not confined to the schedules of Acts but appear in the body of a statute too. There is no difference in principle: delegated legislation can, if Parliament pleases, alter sections as well as schedules. In the old days, before this elastic method had been devised or appreciated, statutes were stiff with rigid detail[1]. Many of the occasions for using the device occur where some uncompromisingly hard-and-fast enactment of an earlier generation requires ad-

---

[1] This disadvantage is admitted by an 1819 Act as to excise duties on plate glass, etc. "Whereas a strict adherence to the regulations established by law for the protection of the revenue in the manufacture of glass has been found by experience greatly to obstruct the preparation and selection of glass" (for optical purposes), the Treasury is authorised to alter the regulations and to prescribe other conditions (59 G. 3, c. 115, s. 4).

justment by modern statute to progressive conditions and a more reasonable pliability. Matters of shillings and pence are seldom specified in a modern Act unless as maximum and minimum limits within which delegated legislation may operate.

Another type of direct amendment is found where the general law is changed and a power is given to adapt or modify any previous statutes so as to make them harmonise with the change. Lord Cave's great Representation of the People Act in 1918 partially introduced the principle of proportional representation and the transferable vote. The Act, in addition to making specific adaptations in a number of previous statutes, delegated a power of adapting the Ballot Act and any other Act relating to parliamentary elections so as to co-ordinate the older law with the new principle[1]. Lord Muir-Mackenzie has stated that delegation of legislative power for this particular purpose "ought not to go so far as to allow the modification of existing Acts of Parliament except in matters of practice and procedure and things of that nature." This opinion was expressed during the House of Lords debate on the Judicial Committee Bill in 1915. That Bill, which made provision for the Privy Council to sit in more than one division at a time, originally contained a power to make statutory rules to include "such adaptations in the enactments relating to the Judicial Committee as may be necessary for giving effect to this Act." Lord Muir-Mackenzie suggested that under such a power the number of the Judicial Committee might be increased or their qualifications altered. This went beyond the intentions of the Bill, and the clause was dropped[2].

It may be added that the power to adapt an Act is sometimes ancillary to the power to apply an Act, of which mention will be made shortly.

B. CREATION OF LEGISLATIVE MACHINERY
(affecting the commencement, duration or application of an Act)

The first example here is the "appointed day clause." When Parliament makes big constitutional or administrative changes, it is convenient to take time over the various stages rather than

---

[1] See 7–8 G. 5, c. 64, s. 20 (3), and its application under the Government of Ireland Act (10–1 G. 5, c. 67, s. 14 (3)).
[2] See Hansard, "Lord's Debates," 1915, vol. xx, pp. 554, 590.

to bring them into force immediately on the passing of the Act or on any hard-and-fast date. Thus we get some such section as this (from the Divorce Act of 1857):

This Act shall come into force on such day not sooner than the first day of January, 1858, as Her Majesty shall by Order in Council appoint....

or this (from the Local Government Act of 1888):

...the appointed day for the purpose of this Act shall...be the first day of April next...or such other day earlier or later as the Local Government Board may appoint....

Such a device is particularly useful and appropriate to the introduction of—

(a) constitutional changes, for example, those made by the Acts which respectively created the Dominion of Canada in 1867, the Commonwealth of Australia in 1900, the Union of South Africa in 1909, and those made by the Government of India Act of 1919 and the Government of Ireland Act of 1920; and

(b) administrative changes, such as those occasioned by the Local Government Acts of 1888 and 1894, the Education Acts of 1902, 1903 and 1918, the Patents and Designs Act of 1919, the establishment of a Public Trustee (see 6 E. 7, c. 55, ss. 1 (1), 14 (1) (a)) or the inter-departmental transfer of powers under the 1919 Acts which created the Ministry of Health[1], the Scottish Board of Health and the Ministry of Transport.

This device of putting an Act on the statute book in a state of suspended animation makes the statute book all the harder for the King's subjects to comprehend. It makes it like a railway time-table issued for normal seasons but upset by a strike. There are the stations and the routes, but are the trains running? The statute book tells us the Acts which Parliament has passed, but we may have to inquire elsewhere to see if the Acts are in force. There is an Act of 1850 (13-4 V. c. 72) about registration of title to land in Ireland which has never come into force yet

[1] See the Ministry of Health Date of Commencement Order printed as an illustration at p. 63 below. For the making of statutory rules under an Act passed but not yet in force, see 52-3 V. c. 63, s. 37.

and now probably never will. The law of Milk and Dairies is as transparently clear as the following complications permit. A little group of Victorian enactments was repealed by an Act of 1914 (4–5 G. 5, c. 49) which was to come into force on such date not later than October 1st, 1915, as the Local Government Board should appoint. This 1914 Act was repealed before it ever came into operation by a 1915 Act (5–6 G. 5, c. 66) which itself has not yet come into force but awaits a day (not later than a year after the end of the war) to be appointed by the Ministry of Health.

All the same, the device has immense administrative value and not a few political advantages. The *fait accompli* of having placed a controversial Act upon the statute book may give great bargaining strength. Not to mention modern instances which will occur to everyone, Henry VIII made good use of it in his fight with Rome. The Act abolishing the payment of first-fruits to Rome was placed upon the statute book in 1532, but it contained a vital section empowering the King—by letters patent to be entered on the Parliament Roll—to give or withhold his assent to the Act or to any parts of it at any time up to Easter 1533[1]. It was a shrewd method of securing diplomatic leverage at a critical moment.

The "appointed day" device can be, and frequently is, elaborated by providing that different days may be appointed for different purposes and for different provisions of the Act, for different areas or parts of areas and for different persons or classes of persons. Part of the Government of India Act of 1919 came into force on January 1st, 1920, other parts on successive dates during April, July and December of that year, while the remainder was finally brought into effect by the beginning of 1921, but on one date for Madras and the Central Provinces, on another for Bihar and Orissa, on a third for Bombay and the rest of India.

The same device which is used for bringing enactments into operation can also be used for revoking them[2]. Sometimes the

---

[1] 23 H. 8, c. 20, s. 4. See preamble to 25 H. 8, c. 20.
[2] For an early instance see 25 H. 8, c. 21, s. 29 (the Act concerning Peter-pence and Dispensations), and the sweeping provisions of 28 H. 8, c. 17 (repeal by successor of Henry VIII on reaching 24 years of age of any statutes passed during his minority).

process of switching on the new law will automatically switch off the old. The power to revoke enactments on some date to be fixed by delegated legislation is especially useful at a time when much temporary and rather experimental law is in force for reasons connected with the war. The provisions temporarily limiting trial by jury and temporarily suspending grand juries were thus made revocable by Order in Council under the Administration of Justice Act, 1920. The Order in Council which decides the official date of the termination of the war helps to repeal a mass of legislation passed for the duration of hostilities only.

This use of delegated legislation for setting statutes in motion or for ending their operation we have classified as "legislative machinery." A similar use is that for the extension and application of Acts. For example the Trade Boards Act of 1909 originally applied to four trades. It was extended to four more by "provisional order," and in 1918 the Minister of Labour was authorised to apply it to yet other trades by "special order," with the result that the Act now applies to over thirty trades. The provisions of the now defunct Profiteering Act were made applicable by Order of the Board of Trade to any article or class of articles or to any process of manufacture, repair, dyeing, cleaning and so on[1].

Such extension is often geographical. There was power, it may be remembered, in the Military Service (No. 2) Act of 1918 to apply that Act by Order in Council to Ireland. Here again great bargaining strength is given by this faculty of applying legislation to particular countries. Under Part II of the Medical Act of 1886 we allow medical men who are duly qualified doctors of foreign countries to practise medicine over here if, in the opinion of the Crown, those foreign countries allow our doctors to practise over there[2]. An Order in Council applied this mutual arrangement to the doctors of Belgium in 1915, but another Order cancelled the concession in 1920, Belgium having ceased to afford to our doctors the privileges of practising in Belgium which they were given during the war. The procedure of applying Acts by Order in Council is an

---

[1] See the Board of Trade Order printed as an illustration at p. 64 below.
[2] 49–50 V. c. 48, ss. 12, 17.

instrument of reciprocity much employed within the Empire. The United Kingdom and the various self-governing Dominions have opportunities of recognising one another's legislation in all sorts of matters—marriages, probates, patents for inventions, enforcement of judgment orders, extradition, solicitors' qualifications and so on. It is as near as we can get to uniformity. We place on the statute book, for example, an Act for the enforcement of judgments reciprocally between the United Kingdom and other parts of His Majesty's Dominions[1], or a Naval Discipline (Dominion Naval Forces) Act in consequence of which the officers of a Dominion Navy may be made interchangeable with the officers of the Royal Navy[2]. As soon as any other nation of the Empire is ready to accept the principle of the Act, an Order in Council seals the bargain.

Occasionally power is delegated to apply whole groups of Acts with modifications. The Foreign Jurisdiction Act of 1890 gives the right to extend a dozen Acts to any foreign country where His Majesty has jurisdiction[3]. There are two remarkable examples of this process. In 1898 an endeavour was being made to fill up some of the gaps which then existed in Irish local government. By a very brief section in a very long Act the Lord Lieutenant was given power to adapt and apply to Ireland by Order in Council any of a large mass of English and Scottish local government Acts mentioned in a schedule[4].

The second example is the Air Force Act of 1917. The authorities wanted an air force distinct from and independent of either Army or Navy. Section 12 of the Air Force (Constitution) Act, 1917, created an Air Force Act consisting of the Army Act with verbal alterations. Section 13 authorised the application by Order in Council to the Air Force of any statute relating to the Army. Under this power more than a hundred Acts have been so applied.

Generally this power to interfere with the machinery of parliamentary legislation (by bringing Acts into operation on "appointed days" or by revoking or applying them) is delegated to His Majesty in Council. Such a course is constitutionally

---

[1] Administration of Justice Act, 1920 (10–1 G. 5, c. 81), part II.
[2] 1–2 G. 5, c. 47.
[3] 53–4 V. c. 37, s. 5, sch. 1.   [4] 61–2 V. c. 37, s. 104, sch. 4.

appropriate in view of the precedents of the sixteenth and seventeenth centuries and in view of Blackstonian theories of the concentration of executive powers in the Crown[1]. But the practice is not uniform. The Board of Education was allowed to fix the appointed days for the 1902, 1903 and 1918 Education Acts and the Governor-General of India in Council was given similar authority as to the Government of India Act, 1919.

C. SUPPLEMENTARY LEGISLATION

Instances of the delegation of power to make rules, regulations and orders which elaborate, supplement or help to work out some principle which Parliament has laid down, hardly need to be quoted. It is common to leave subsidiary matters to be settled by subsidiary legislation. Tables of fees of all kinds, postal rates, scales of railway charges, the prescribing of various forms, and especially the framing of judicial procedure[2]—all these are appropriate for delegation if there is an authority to which Parliament can confidently delegate them. The province of Parliament, said a great parliamentary counsel[3], is to decide material questions affecting the public interest; and the more procedure and subordinate matters can be withdrawn from their cognizance, the greater will be the time afforded for the consideration of the more serious questions involved in legislation.

One cannot quite say that all major matters of permanent legislative importance are dealt with by Parliament itself and that all minor matters of temporary importance are delegated. Many of the matters which are delegated are of first-rate importance. Procedure may be all-important. A practising barrister or solicitor had better know the Rules of the Supreme Court than the Judicature Acts under which they are made. An officer on court-martial duty may find the Rules of Procedure almost as valuable as the Army Act itself. A very few

[1] In Blackstone's day the eye of the law saw the king only. Secretaries of State and heads of departments were not "the objects of our laws"; modern statutes talk freely of Ministers and Boards and Departments. See Maitland, "Constitutional Law," p. 415, commenting on Blackstone, bk 1, c. ix.

[2] For a study of rule-making in the judicial courts of the Empire see an article by S. Rosenbaum in the "Journal of the Society of Comparative Legislation," vol. xv, p. 128.

[3] Thring, "Practical Legislation," p. 13.

examples will show that vitally important matters are delegated.

During 1920 a Seeds Act was passed to provide that purchasers of seeds should be furnished with written particulars
of what they are buying, to provide for the taking and testing
of samples, and generally to prevent the sale of bad seeds.
Parliament did not trouble to go into details. It did not even
decide what kind of seeds it was legislating for. It was content
to pass this section:

The Minister may, after consultation with representatives of the
interests concerned...make regulations generally for the purpose of
carrying this Act into effect, and in particular...for prescribing the
seeds...to which this Act is to apply.

That is what Lord Herschell called skeleton legislation[1]. The
Act is a kind of preliminary announcement of legislation.
Across it there might be stamped the words: "For Particulars
see Small Hand Bills." Parliament has had a legislative idea,
has sketched an outline, has laid down a principle—and has left
it at that. There are safeguards, which will be discussed in a
future chapter; but in the main Parliament has turned over to
the technical advisers and the permanent administrative staff of
the Ministry of Agriculture the business of making the Seeds
Act a practical part of our law. Here is another example, the
Air Navigation Act, 1920. It begins by saying that His Majesty
may make such Orders in Council as appear to him necessary
for carrying out a convention signed at Paris in October, 1919,
"for determining by a common agreement certain uniform
rules with respect to international air navigation." Section 3
enumerates a dozen or more matters which an Order in Council
may provide for. They include the licensing, inspection and
regulation of aerodromes and landing-places, the issue, sus-
pension and endorsement of licences, the conditions under
which mails, passengers and goods can be carried by air, aerial
lighthouses and signalling, general safety regulations and penalties for breach of any of these provisions. Under the Roads
Act, passed at the same date, the Ministry of Transport receives
power to make regulations generally for the purpose of carrying

[1] See [1894] A.C. at p. 356.

the Act into effect, and in particular as to registration of motor-vehicles, size, shape and character of identification marks, where they are to be fixed and so on. These are not ungenerous delegations of legislative power. The result for the aviator or the motorist is that the statute book contains but a fraction of the actual law he wants to know. It is the same elsewhere. There are Acts about such matters as cremation, cinematograph shows, convict prisons, police discipline and so on which have left most of the important points to be dealt with by regulations of the Home Secretary. Not to multiply instances further, there are masses of statutory rules and orders about education, housing, national health insurance and unemployment insurance without which nobody can understand the law and administration of those subjects[1]. Our administrative law is mostly statutory and is constantly being modernised; it is increasingly dependent on the statutory rule and order system. It is not suggested that the consequent insufficiency of the statute book is in any way improper or unconstitutional. Parliament can do what it likes. When Parliament legislates at high pressure and when there is hardly time to think out how an Act is going to work, it is natural to delegate wide general powers of making rules and regulations "for carrying this Act into effect."

The collection is so vast that it is difficult to choose representative specimens and the description of it becomes a mere catalogue, but there are just two other pieces of delegated legislation which we must find room to mention.

There used to be an Aliens Act of 1905 which imposed a number of restrictions upon aliens. A later Act of 1919 gave His Majesty in Council power to repeal the 1905 Act but to incorporate any of its provisions in an Order in Council. Though, apart from this, there are various statutory provisions about aliens, this delegation by Parliament to the King in Council is a remarkable surrender. But, after all, it may be supposed that neither Parliament nor the country cared very much in 1919 how aliens were regulated so long as they were regulated. And, historically the

---

[1] For the general effect of subordinate legislation in local government see an article by Mr A. S. Quekett, L.Q.R. (1918), xxxiv, pp. 364–9.

regulation and control of aliens is one of the matters in which the King in Council had anciently an especial concern[1]. Aliens were a kind of royal perquisite in mediaeval times.

The last example of all to be quoted is the one which will already have occurred to everybody—the delegation of legislative power for the Defence of the Realm during the great war. Here the initial parliamentary legislation was slight, a mere pronouncement that His Majesty in Council had power to issue regulations during the war for securing the public safety and the defence of the Realm. In submitting a brief Bill to the House of Commons on August 7th, 1914, the Home Secretary made a speech of barely a hundred words which merely indicated the desirability of having some speedy means of trying offences "in cases of tapping wires or attempts to blow up bridges." From this grain of mustard seed sprang a goodly forest of regulations. Once again we have to notice that the statute book here gives no hint of the nature of the legislation which it empowered. Who could have foreseen at the beginning that the Defence of the Realm Regulations would have embraced the acquisition of factories, the appropriation of materials, such as hay, wool or flax, the control of food supply and food production, the disposal of securities, the felling of timber and the taking over of mines, railways, shipping and the liquor industry? Who would have guessed that those regulations would be extended to prohibit the holding of dog-shows, the sale of opium or the whistling for cabs in London,—all in the name of the Defence of the Realm[2]? The Consolidating Act (5–6 G. 5, c. 8) did something to outline the scope of the regulations; so does the similar Restoration of Order in Ireland Act of 1920. But there is nothing in these Acts to tell the citizen what he must do. The greater the emergency, the wider the delegation of legislative power, and the more incomplete the statute book.

---

[1] Compare with a modern Aliens Order, the commands to the Lombards in 1426 (to write their foreign correspondence in plain language, not in cipher: not to enter the Realm without passport, etc.): "Proceedings of Privy Council," I, p. 289.

[2] As to this see Lord Cave in the "Contemporary Review" for Jan., 1920, at p. 35, and Mr S. W. Clarke in the "Journal of the Society of Comparative Legislation," 3rd series, vol. I, pt I. The former inclines to regard D.O.R.A. as on the whole a benevolent despot.

CHAPTER III

THE CASE FOR DELEGATION

IN addition to the administrative advantages of which mention has already been made, there are three main justifications for the delegation of legislative power by Parliament.

The first is the plain fact that Parliament simply has not time to do otherwise. There was leisure in that mediaeval Parliament of Estates when grievances were submitted and were referred to the appropriate authority. There was leisure in the Tudor and Stuart times when Crown and Parliament fought over privilege and prerogative. There was leisure even in that third period which ran from 1688 to the Reform Act of 1832 when the party system was elaborated and the Cabinet became part of our constitution. During that period a few great Acts were passed, the Bill of Rights, the Act of Settlement, the Union with Scotland and with Ireland, the Septennial Act and so on, but there was as yet, no popular demand for legislation.

From 1832 onwards, the leisure began to disappear. The stages are recounted by Professor Redlich and summarised by Sir Courtenay Ilbert[1]. The new franchise introduced the middle classes to their share in legislation and administration. Constituencies became more exacting; politicians became more conscious of the importance of being earnest. Speakers increased in number and speeches in length. Gladstone had known the time when Parliament rose at half-past six of an afternoon and everyone went home for the evening with a sense of duty done. Parnell and the obstructionists altered all that. They studied the details of the working of an always cumbrous machine in order to find out how best to delay its action and throw it out of gear. Meanwhile the machine was being constantly called upon to do more work. Administration grew more complex. The State intervened more and more in domestic

---

[1] See Redlich, "Procedure of the House of Commons," with introduction by Sir C. P. Ilbert.

affairs. Imperial problems exacted attention. Various shifts were devised for economising parliamentary time. Legislation occupies only a part of that time, but it was possible to diminish its demands. The invention and extension of the "provisional order" and "special order" procedure, the birth of the group of "clauses Acts" in 1845, the process of substituting a general or permanent Act for a series of particular or periodical Acts— all these have brought some relief. But as long ago as 1877 Lord Thring, then parliamentary counsel, said that the adoption of a system of confining the attention of Parliament to material provisions only, and leaving details to be settled departmentally, was probably the only way in which parliamentary government could, as respects its legislative functions, be carried on[1]. And to-day, even when a substantial party majority has facilitated the working of the parliamentary machine, there is less leisure than ever. Some may note an increasing inclination to find in fresh legislation a remedy for all national ills, and an increasing tendency to expect Parliament to intervene in industrial crises. No one who looks at a collection of the annual output of delegated legislation can seriously propose that Parliament should now cancel the concession of legislative power and should undertake for the future under its own direct authority all the legislative activities which at present are left to His Majesty in Council or to the various public departments.

Next to the limitation of parliamentary time comes another limitation—to be mentioned more diffidently—the limitation of aptitude. John Stuart Mill, the candid friend of Representative Government, considered it impossible that the conditions proper to law-making could be fulfilled when laws are voted clause by clause by a miscellaneous assembly, though, as he went on to observe, our laws are already such a chaos in form and construction that the confusion and contradiction cannot be made worse by any addition. If Parliament nevertheless manages to get through a great deal of successful legislating, it is inadequately equipped for dealing with some of the technical matters which are brought before it. There are experts in the House of Commons but on many matters such as patents, copy-

---

[1] "Practical Legislation," p. 13.

right, trade marks, designs, diseases, poisons, the pattern of miners' safety lamps, wireless telegraphy, the heating and lighting values of gas, legal procedure or the intricacies of finance, the House would probably be content to lay down general principles and to leave details to the departments which specialise in those subjects. It is the national habit to distrust experts. To place a soldier in charge of the War Office, a doctor at the Ministry of Health and a railway manager at the Ministry of Transport was an audacious experiment which nothing but Armageddon would have led us into. Lord Bryce says somewhere[1] that our democratic system "makes the people self-confident, and that self-confidence may easily pass into a jealousy of delegated power, an undervaluing of skill and knowledge, a belief that any citizen is good enough for any political work." But the House of Commons knows its limitations. As a typical example of the way in which pressure of time and disinclination to discuss technicalities have led Parliament to lay down a principle and to leave details to others, we may notice the Sex Disqualification (Removal) Act of 1919. The principle of equality of sex is boldly laid down, but two obvious difficulties in working out the principle—the arrangements for jury service by women, and the position of women in the civil service—are left to be dealt with by rules and regulations.

And now we come to the third and greatest justification for delegated legislation. Parliament authorises taxation, provides money for administration, appropriates the money to particular purposes, and criticises the way the money goes. But Parliament does not govern the country. The country is governed by the executive, i.e. the Ministers of the Crown responsible to and appointed by Parliament. Those Ministers depend on parliamentary support. They must have Parliament behind them at every step. But Parliament is not always in existence[2], and, if in existence it is not always sitting; even when it is in Session its procedure is slow. Crises arrive when the Government of the country must act quickly without waiting for Parliament.

[1] "The American Commonwealth," II, p. 636.
[2] Professor Jenks in a letter to "The Times" (April 5, 1921) has suggested that the Emergency Powers Act, 1920, overlooks this contingency.

While a crisis endures, it may be necessary to ignore constitutional rights and to curtail traditional liberties. The restoration of law and order or the preservation of life and health may be more important than Magna Carta and the Habeas Corpus Act. The problem then is how to reconcile the acts of the executive with the supremacy of ·Parliament, how to compensate the government of the country for the loss of the prerogative powers which have lapsed or been taken away. It is possible, of course, to make everything smooth by a subsequent Act of Indemnity. The other method is to anticipate the difficulties and to delegate the power to deal with them promptly. In the days when Parliament explained its objects in preambles—contemporary documents of high historical value—there was no hesitation in admitting that there were sudden emergencies with which the normal resources and machinery of Parliament were unfitted to cope.

The first of these confessions is to be found in Henry VIII's famous Statute of Proclamations[1]. "Considering," says the preamble,

that sudden causes and occasions fortune many times which do require speedy remedies and that by abiding for a Parliament in the meantime might happen great prejudice to ensue to the Realm... it is therefore thought in manner more than necessary that the King's Highness of this Realm for the time being with the advice of his honourable Council should make and set forth proclamations for the good and politic order and governance of this his Realm...for the defence of his regal dignity and the advancement of his commonwealth and good quiet of his people as the cases of necessity shall require.

James I, in answering the Petition of Grievances in 1610 followed the same line. He had to admit that proclamations had not the same force as law:

yet nevertheless we think it a duty appertaining to us and inseparately annexed to our crown and royal authority to restrain and prevent such mischiefs and inconveniences as We see growing in the Common Weal against which no certain law is extant and which may tend to the great grief and prejudice of Our subjects if there should be no remedy provided until a Parliament; which prerogative Our progenitors have, as well in ancient as latter times, used and enjoyed[2].

[1] 31 H. 8, c. 8.   [2] S.P. Dom. James I, LVI, 40.

In a proclamation issued on September 24th he repeated his claim to apply speedy, proper and convenient remedies in all cases of sudden and extraordinary accidents and in matters so variable and irregular in their nature as are not provided for by law nor can fitly fall under the certain rule of a law[1].

Even Coke admitted that "in all cases the King out of his providence and to prevent dangers which it will be too late to prevent afterwards, may prohibit them before, which will aggravate the offence if it be afterwards committed[2]." This would give the King power to issue proclamations pending legislation. It is perhaps in this connection that James in 1610 excused some of his proclamations as "intended to be but temporary."

Henry and James agree as to the disadvantage of waiting for a Parliament in a sudden emergency. But whereas Henry uses the principle in order to obtain powers from Parliament, James uses it in order to exclude Parliament altogether.

Henry, who sometimes drafted preambles with his own hand, made Parliament confess its difficulty. Long afterwards when the struggle between King and Commons was over, Parliament was willing to make the confession again. In 1710 there had been plague in the Baltic, and Anne had been obliged to impose quarantine precautions by proclamation. But there was difficulty about punishing persons who offended against proclamations which had no statutory authority, for by this time it was settled law that a proclamation cannot of itself create a new offence. An Act was therefore passed to authorise the Queen to make orders, rules and directions about quarantine and to notify them by proclamation. This provision was expressly made to enforce quarantine "in a more expeditious manner than at present can be in the ordinary methods of the law[3]." The same purpose underlies the legislation passed in the cholera epidemic of 1832[4]. The preamble admits that Parliament may not be able to act quickly enough.

Whereas it has pleased Almighty God to visit the United Kingdom with the disease called the cholera or spasmodic or Indian cholera,

---

[1] S.P. Dom. James I, LVII, p. 236.   [2] Co. Rep. XII, 75.
[3] 9 Anne, c. 2. See the three proclamations (1710 Nov. 9, 1711 Sept. 6 and 1712 Aug. 31) catalogued by Mr Steele in the "Bibliotheca Lindesiana."
[4] 2 W. 4, c. 10.

and whereas, with a view to prevent as far as may be possible by the Divine Blessing the spreading of the said disease, it may be necessary that rules and regulations may from time to time be established within cities, towns or districts affected with or which may be threatened by the said disease, but it may be impossible to establish such rules and regulations by the authority of Parliament with sufficient promptitude to meet the exigency of any such case as it may occur

—therefore it is enacted that the Privy Council may make such rules and regulations for preventing the spread of the disease, relieving the sufferers and burying the dead. This Act, though there may have been earlier examples, was a pattern for subsequent public health measures. The Privy Council's Orders were to be published in the " Gazette," a copy of which was to be evidence of them; and they were to be laid before Parliament. The Orders when made, ranged from a direction that vessels with cholera aboard should hoist a yellow flag to provisions for special prayers.

Fifteen years later the weapon forged for the fight against plague and cholera was used against other diseases. Parliament repeats in the same terms the justification of sudden emergency and again apologises, as it were, for its own slowness of movement.

Whereas cases may occur where cities, towns or places may be threatened with or affected by formidable contagious or epidemic diseases and it may be impossible to establish rules for the prevention thereof by the authority of Parliament with sufficient promptitude to meet the exigency of each case,...it is therefore expedient to enable the Lords of Her Majesty's Most Honourable Privy Council to issue orders in England and Scotland and the Lord Lieutenant and Privy Council of Ireland to issue orders in Ireland from time to time for that purpose[1].

Soon afterwards in 1848 similar power was delegated under the first of the Contagious Diseases of Animals Acts[2]. Parliament had by this time given up apologising for delegating its legislative duties, nor did it think any express justification need be recorded in a preamble when in 1877 the device which had been found so useful in combating the diseases of men and of

---

[1] 9–10 V. c. 96, s. 5. Contrast 59 G. 3, c. 41, an Act "to establish regulations for preventing contagious diseases in Ireland"; the Act contains its own regulations and delegates no legislative power.
[2] 11–2 V. c. 105, ss. 105, 107.

animals was extended also to protect the vegetable kingdom
from the attacks of the Colorado Beetle[1]. For fighting this and
other "destructive insects and pests"—the Gooseberry Mildew,
Gipsy Moth, Onion Smut and the rest of the army of pesti-
ferous invaders—orders have been constantly made, though the
Ministry of Agriculture now exercises the powers instead of
the Privy Council[2]. Where human diseases are concerned, the
recently created Ministry of Health justifies its title by exer-
cising the powers of the Privy Council under the modern Acts
which supersede those early statutes which we have quoted.

In the earlier days, when there was as yet neither a Health
Ministry nor a Local Government Board specially concerned
with health matters[3], it was natural that the power (half legislative and half executive) of making orders to deal with epi-
demics should be vested in the Privy Council. Once the
machinery was set up, the system of delegated legislation which
was essential for a sudden emergency could be used for recur-
rent or intermittent danger to public health. In 1858 the Privy
Council was authorised to make regulations for the efficient
performance of vaccination. In 1889 the power to make dog-
muzzling orders gave the country a long immunity from rabies.
Delegated legislation may be proud of its record as the servant
of medical science. A country which could not allow itself so
useful a weapon may well envy us. Sir Frederick Pollock has
hinted that the Gipsy Moth's ravages have created constitutional misgivings in one of the United States of America[4].

The influence of emergency upon legislation manifests itself
in three examples within the memory of all. The crisis of
August 1914 which brought forth the Defence of the Realm
Act; the difficulties of August 1920 when the Restoration of
Order in Ireland Act was passed; and the occasion, two months
later, when "exceptional provision" was made "for the pro-

[1] 40–1 V. c. 68, s. 1.
[2] 7 E. 7, c. 4, s. 1. In the case of forest trees or timber, the Forestry
Commissioners exercise the power (see 9–10 G. 5, c. 58, s. 3 (2)).
[3] By 1848 (see 11–2 V. c. 63 and 11–2 V. c. 123, s. 9) there was a General
Board of Health with rule-making power. Its powers passed to the Privy
Council in 1858, thence to the Local Government Board in 1871, and so to
the Ministry of Health in 1919.
[4] "The Genius of the Common Law," p. 43.

tection of the community in cases of emergency." If the State is threatened with new perils, it may have to take new weapons. If the Emergency Powers Act of 1920 was merely prospective, the prospect was not so very remote. The war had shown the country many holes in its armour. The Defence of the Realm Regulations contained many provisions which we have been glad to incorporate in our permanent law. They also contained much which could not be finally jettisoned if hostilities against enemy nations were to be succeeded by hostilities at home. The condition which made the grant of emergency powers contingent upon the prior declaration of a state of emergency, offers of course some material to critics, since everybody will not always agree as to what is an emergency. The well-to-do classes may see one approaching when the criminal classes are sceptical. But the nation knows an emergency when it sees it, and knows how it should be met. The Defence of the Realm Regulations, the Restoration of Order in Ireland Regulations, and the Emergency Powers Regulations may have been criticised on points of detail, and still more on points of execution. But there are few people who will say that something of the kind was not essential.

If this be true, then delegated legislation has justified itself. Its critics may say it has been abused. They have not yet said that it should be abolished. If it did not exist, it would be necessary to invent it, as the United States of America discovered during the war[1]. But countries will suffer in war-time diminutions of liberty which they will not permit during peace. Delegated legislation is no permanent substitute for Parliamentary legislation. A prominent Irish politician won the approval of all sides when he observed in the House of Commons: "You cannot govern Ireland by Orders in Council[2]." In so far as delegated legislation contains the germ of arbitrary administration, every possible safeguard must be devised.

[1] "The President's executive powers have been further enlarged in recent years by the growing practice on the part of Congress of passing laws in general terms, which laws have to be supplemented by regulations drawn up by the head of a department under the direction of the President....It used to be said that ' Congress may not delegate its powers'; but the rule nowadays has become that Congress may not delegate its powers unless it is convenient to do so." Prof. E. S. Corwin, "The Constitution and what it means to-day," p. 62.   [2] Hansard, "Commons Debates," June 3, 1920, pp. 2117, 2145.

CHAPTER IV

SAFEGUARDS

IF Parliament passes an Act which we do not like, we have, in theory, only ourselves to thank. We were all of us theoretically represented at the passing of the Act. We were all of us vicariously present at Westminster and we knew all about it. How otherwise could we explain the rule that Acts of Parliament take effect without being promulgated[1]? If Parliament passes an Act which we do not like, our remedy is to get the Act repealed or amended. If our representatives obstruct us in this course, we must see that others are elected at the first opportunity.

Now if delegated legislation is made which we do not like, what is our remedy? If it is the fact of the delegation which we find objectionable, we must press as before for the repeal or amendment of the Act which brought it about. The concession which Parliament gave, Parliament can of course take away.

Were a regulation to be framed......to intern the Catholics of Ireland or the Jews of London, the result would, I think, be the speedy repeal of the Act which authorised the legislation[2].

Lord Dunedin was putting an extreme case. If it is not a question of flatly revoking the delegation of legislative power, but merely of confining the operation of that power within proper limits, how are we to ensure that the concession is not abused? What safeguards have we against the making of objectionable statutory rules and orders? What conditions ought we to insist upon?

We want five things particularly.

(1) The delegation of legislative power should be delegation to a trustworthy authority which commands the national confidence.

---

[1] See the Bishop of Chichester's case, Y.B. 39 Edw. 3, f. 7: Smith, "De Republica Anglorum," bk II, c. 1: Blackstone, 1 Comm. 185: and Lord Hardwicke in *Middleton* v. *Croft*, Strange, 1056.

[2] Per Lord Dunedin, *R.* v. *Halliday* [1917] A.C. at p. 271.

As has already been suggested, the grant of legislative power by royal charter to towns, merchant companies and craft gilds or fellowships indicates that we are traditionally disposed to countenance a pretty wide delegation. Charters of incorporation from the time of Elizabeth onwards contain an explicit clause empowering the making of laws and ordinances "for better government" and it will not be forgotten that Coke declared that the power to make bye-laws was one of the incidental provisions "*tacite* annexed" to a grant of corporateness[1]. From the delegation of legislative power to trading corporations by royal charter, we have proceeded to delegation of bye-law-making power to limited companies under the Companies Acts. The same process is visible elsewhere. Universities, colleges and municipal corporations now have statutory authority to make statutes and bye-laws. Royal charters are by no means dead, but Parliament has largely supplanted the Crown as the giver of law-making power. Whether the power has been given by the prerogative or by Act of Parliament, the significant fact is that the delegation has been generous and that the generosity has not been altogether abused. If that be true of subordinate and local bodies, it should be not less true of Government departments or of the King in Council. As Lord Herschell said in discussing the delegation by Parliament to the Board of Trade of power to make rules about patent agents, "it is a very large power...but it is committed to a public department and a public department largely under the control of Parliament itself[2]." In times of great public danger, great powers may be entrusted to His Majesty in Council, and Parliament may entrust those powers "feeling certain that such powers will be reasonably exercised[3]." Public departments are trusted to exercise the powers in the public interest, while the subject who thinks he is oppressed is left to his proper remedies for an oppressive use by the executive of their legal powers[4]. Parliament "risks the chance of abuse[5]."

[1] Sutton's Hospital Case, Co. Rep. x, 30 *b*, 31 *a*.
[2] *Institute of Patent Agents* v. *Lockwood* [1894] A.C. at p. 357.
[3] Per Lord Findlay L.C., *R.* v. *Halliday* [1917] A.C. at pp. 268–9.
[4] See judgment of Atkin J., *Lipton Ltd* v. *Ford* [1917] 2 K.B. at p. 654.
[5] Per Lord Atkinson, *R.* v. *Halliday* [1917] A.C. at p. 271.

(2) The limits within which the delegated power is to be exercised ought to be definitely laid down.

Not the least of safeguards is the certainty that our Courts of Law can be moved to declare that any overstepping of those limits is *ultra vires*. Such declarations were valuable enough before 1914 where a railway company or a limited company or a secondary law-making body of any kind went too far in its legislation. The war brought a fresh crop of cases, more important because the delegation of legislative power was more wide and because personal liberty was the more gravely imperilled. In passing the Defence of the Realm Act of 1914 Parliament imposed only two conditions on the making of regulations thereunder. The regulations must in the first place be made during the war. In the second place they must purport to be made for the purpose of securing the public safety and the defence of the Realm; if they could not in any reasonable way aid that purpose, then they might be challenged as *ultra vires* and therefore void. The constitutional result of this almost unrestricted delegation was remarkable. Normally it is for Parliament to legislate and for the executive to govern. If Parliament delegates legislative power to the executive, then both the legislative and the executive functions are in the same hands. The dissenting judgment delivered by Lord Shaw of Dunfermline in *Rex* v. *Halliday*[1] states the consequent danger.

The form in modern times of using the Privy Council as the executive channel for statutory power is measured, and must be measured strictly, by the ambit of the legislative pronouncement. That channel itself, seeing that under the constitution His Majesty acts only through his ministers is simply the Government of the day. The author of the power is Parliament; the wielder of it is the Government. Whether the Government has exceeded its statutory mandate is a question *ultra* or *intra vires*.... In so far as the mandate has been exceeded, there lurk the elements of a transition to arbitrary Government and therein of grave constitutional and public danger. The increasing crush of legislative efforts and the convenience to the executive of a refuge to the device of Orders in Council would increase that danger tenfold were the judiciary to approach any action of the Government in a spirit of compliance rather than of independent scrutiny. That way also would lie public unrest and public peril.

[1] Ib. p. 287.

If anybody was to blame for the fact that the executive thus acquired dangerous powers, Parliament at least was not innocent. By the Defence of the Realm legislation Parliament left it to executive officers to decide whether a particular action was or was not necessary for the successful prosecution of the war. It was not fair to expect the judiciary to review the decision.

Those who are responsible for the national security must be the sole judges of what the national security requires. It would be obviously undesirable that such matters should be made the subject of evidence in a Court of law or otherwise discussed in public[1].

And in spite of the perils to which Lord Shaw drew attention, it was too late to speak of Magna Carta and the Habeas Corpus Acts.

Magna Carta has not remained untouched. Like every other law of England it is not condemned to that immunity from development or improvement which was attributed to the laws of the Medes and Persians[2].

However precious the personal liberty of the subject may be, there is something for which it may well be to some extent sacrificed by legal enactment, namely national success in the war or escape from national plunder or enslavement[3].

If the legislature chooses to enact a deprivation of liberty which conflicts with Habeas Corpus Acts or Magna Carta, the enactment or orders made thereunder—if *intra vires*—do not infringe upon the Habeas Corpus Acts or Magna Carta for the simple reason that the new legislation and the Orders made under it have become part of the law of the land. It is, as Professor Pollard has observed[4], a modern myth that Englishmen have always been consumed with enthusiasm for parliamentary government and with a thirst for a parliamentary vote. They will fight for their liberties; but, when Englishmen overseas are sacrificing their lives for their country, other Englishmen at home will not mind sacrificing some of their liberty. Shakespeare could write a play about King John without mentioning Magna Carta.

As Parliament had not conceded to the executive during the war an absolutely unlimited power of legislation, the law courts

---

[1] Per Lord Parker, *The Zamora* [1916] 2 A.C. at p. 106. See the protest of Scrutton L.J., in *Ronnfeldt* v. *Phillips* [1918] 35 T.L.R. at p. 47.
[2] Per Darling J., *Chester* v. *Bateson* [1920] 1 K.B. at p. 832.
[3] Per Lord Atkinson, *R.* v. *Halliday* [1917] A.C. at pp. 271–2.
[4] "Henry VIII," pp. 24–5.

still were able to insist that the exercise of the subordinate legislative power should not exceed the limits which Parliament had laid down. Several of the regulations made under the Defence of the Realm Act were challenged as *ultra vires*. A regulation empowering the Secretary of State to order the internment of any person of hostile origin or associations, where on the recommendation of a competent naval or military authority it appeared to him expedient for securing the public safety or defence of the Realm, was challenged and upheld in *Rex* v. *Halliday*[1]. A regulation taking possession of a crop of raspberries was challenged and upheld in *Lipton Ltd* v. *Ford*[2]. Regulations under which the Shipping Controller ordered vessels to load cargoes and to carry them between named ports at fixed rates of freightage were upheld in *Hudson's Bay Co.* v. *Maclay*[3], even though hostilities were over and German submarines were powerless. On the other hand a regulation that no person should without the consent of the Ministry of Munitions take proceedings to recover possession of a house so long as a war-worker was living in it, was held in *Chester* v. *Bateson*[4] to be *ultra vires* and void. It might have been necessary to the public safety that munitions should be made and that munition-workers should be housed, but not that a minister should thus have power to forbid under pain of fine and imprisonment the institution of such proceedings.

Finally a regulation purporting to deprive persons whose goods were requisitioned of their right to fair market value and to a judicial decision of the amount was held to be *ultra vires* in *Newcastle Breweries* v. *The King*[5].

These examples suffice to show that even in moments of emergency, if Parliament will set some definite limits to the exercise of delegated power, the judiciary will furnish a safeguard by seeing that these limits are observed[6].

(3) In the third place, if any particular interests are to be specially affected by delegated legislation, the legislating authority should consult them before making its laws.

---

[1] [1917] A.C. 260.   [2] [1917] 2 K.B. 647.   [3] (1920) 36 T.L.R. 469.
[4] [1920] 1 K.B. 829.   [5] [1920] 1 K.B. 854.
[6] For a case in which Parliament afterwards ratified an *ultra vires* use of delegated legislation, see *A.-G.* v. *Brown* [1920] 1 K.B. 773 and 10–1 G. 5, c. 48, s. 4. Compare 48 G. 3, c. 37 and 53 G. 3, c. 12.

Parliament can do much to ensure that such interests are consulted. We have seen for example[1], that the Ministry of Agriculture, before making any regulations under the Seeds Act, is to consult "representatives of the interests concerned." The Board of Trade, which possesses wide powers (exercised either directly by itself or indirectly through the Privy Council) of potential interference with commerce, was equipped by Act of Parliament with an Advisory Committee of "persons concerned in the trades of dye-maker or dye-user" for the purposes of the Dyestuffs (Import Regulation) Act, 1920, and with an advisory committee of twenty-four persons representing elaborately specified interests for the purposes of the Mining Industry Act, 1920. The Minister of Transport has been given advisory committees on rates, on harbour charges, on roads and on tramways. The Ministry of Agriculture, the Board of Education and the Electricity Commissioners all have statutory councils and committees which they can consult. Even if no such statutory provision were made, it is improbable that a department would be wholly out of touch with the interests concerned. Indeed the country is as likely to reproach it with listening too carefully to those interests as with not listening at all.

Before the Minister of Labour makes a Special Order applying the Trade Boards Act to some fresh trade, he must publish notice of his intention "in such manner as he thinks best adapted for informing persons affected" and must consider any objections thereupon submitted and hold a public enquiry if the objections are not merely frivolous. Without enumerating particular examples of the same kind, there are the general provisions of section 1 of the Rules Publication Act of 1893 which try to prevent legislation being made without regard to the interests concerned. A short account of the genesis of this Act is necessary in order to explain its limitations[2].

In 1890 the President of the Incorporated Law Society announced that the Council had prepared a Bill to provide that new rules of the Supreme Courts and County Courts should be

---

[1] See p. 16, above.
[2] This account of the Bill is gathered from the contemporary pages of Hansard and the "Solicitors' Journal."

published for a specified time before sanction so as to afford a chance for criticism and suggestion. The solicitors may have felt aggrieved by the making of rules over their heads, for it was not till 1893 that the Lord Chancellor suggested adding the President of the Law Society and also a practising barrister to the Rules Committee, and it was not till 1909 that Parliament actually did include practising barristers and solicitors amongst the members of the Rules Committee.

In 1890 then a Rules Publication Bill was brought forward. In 1891 it got its first reading, but was held up because the Attorney-General thought such a Bill should not be confined to legal rules only. The proposals were therefore modified so as to apply to the rules of all Government Departments[1], and the consequent antagonism of those Departments—according to its supporters—was fatal. In 1893 the Bill was brought up again. Its sponsors claimed that they now had letters from all Government Departments assenting to the principle. It passed the Commons, but in the Lords several exemptions crept in, together with a new clause (afterwards section 3) as to the numbering, printing and sale of rules whereof more anon.

At the end of 1893 the Rules Publication Act received the royal assent[2]. Its main provision for our present purpose was the first section which enacted that, wherever any statute authorised the making of statutory rules[3] and directed the laying of those rules before Parliament, at least forty days' notice must be given in the "London Gazette" (or, in the case of Irish rules, in the "Irish Gazette") of the proposal to make the rules, and of the place where copies could be obtained. Any public body could thus get a copy and make representations or suggestions in writing which the rule-making authority would have to take into consideration before making the rules in their final form.

This provision was not an entirely novel device. The Parliamentary Counsel's Office had long known it as a safeguard appropriate to particular cases. Sir Henry Thring had observed

---

[1] The original restriction to legal rules and the subsequent extension to departmental rules stands on record in the definition clause in section 4 of the Act (see p. 45 below) and explains its limited application.

[2] The Act is printed for convenient reference in Appendix I, at p. 57 below.

[3] "Statutory rules" in s. 1 do not, it seems, include orders.

in 1877 that "any attempt to evade the vigilance of Parliament by relegating to departments important matters can always be prevented by requiring the rules made to be laid before Parliament before they come into force[1]." What was novel was the attempted standardisation of procedure and the general application. That application was nevertheless not universal. Several departments, with which the proposals may be assumed to have been unpopular, were exempted altogether—the Local Government Board for England (the various powers of which have now been transferred to the Ministry of Health and other departments), the Local Government Board for Ireland, the Board of Trade, the Revenue Departments and the Post Office. Rules made by the Board (now the Ministry) of Agriculture under the Contagious Diseases (Animals) Acts were also excepted[2]. This part of the Rules Publication Act was therefore of partial application only. It did not apply to Scotland at all, nor to any rules made under any Act which requires rules or draft rules to be laid before Parliament for any period before they come into operation. And in a number of cases since 1893 particular statutory rules have been excepted from section 1 of the Act[3].

It is essential to distinguish between a safeguard which is ante-natal and a safeguard which is post-natal. The provisions of section 1 of the Rules Publication Act (as to notifying the proposal to make rules) we may call ante-natal; section 1 takes effect at a time when the statutory rule is not yet born but is merely thought of. The provisions of section 3 (as to publishing rules when made) we may call post-natal; section 3—with which we shall deal in the next chapter—does not operate until a valid rule has actually been born.

To recapitulate the scope of section 1, the requirement that forty days' notice must be given of the proposal to make rules applies only where a statute has directed that a rule is to be laid before Parliament. Thus the Rules of the Supreme Court which have to be laid before Parliament fall within section 1, whereas

---

[1] "Practical Legislation," p. 13.
[2] See section 1 (4) at p. 57 below.
[3] See the list of Acts tabulated in the third column opposite 56–7 V. c. 66 in the official Chronological Table of All the Statutes.

the County Court Rules which have to be submitted to the Lord Chancellor instead do not[1].

Further, when an Act directs that rules made under it are to be laid before Parliament, there are still two cases in which section 1 does not apply, namely,

(a) where the rule-making department or the rules concerned are expressly excepted under s. 1 (4), or

(b) where the statute under which the rule is made itself makes independent provision for the ante-natal safeguard of laying rules before Parliament for any period before they come into operation[2].

There is yet another loop-hole of escape from the provisions of section 1, a loop-hole left to meet occasions when emergency or urgency make the delay of the quarantine period undesirable. Section 2 of the Act says that, where a rule-making authority certifies that on account of urgency or any special reason any rule should come into immediate operation, the authority may make such rules as "provisional rules," in which case they shall have effect only until rules are made in accordance with the earlier provisions of the Act. It was doubtless intended that a department which could not wait forty days and which therefore made its rules as "provisional" should convert its provisional rules into substantive rules by the statutory process already described. This is usually so done[3]. Thus the Ministry of Health, having to issue its regulations under the Census Act of 1920 in a hurry as preparations had to be rapidly made for the 1921 census, certified its regulations as urgent and issued them as "provisional" on December 21st, 1920, and followed them up by producing draft rules three days later which went through the quarantine period and came permanently into force on February 14th, 1921[4]. But, once rules have been made

---

[1] See 38–9 V. c. 77, ss. 17, 25 and 51–2 V. c. 43, s. 164 (1). This explanation removes the uncertainty expressed by Mr S. Rosenbaum in L.Q.R. (1915), XXXI, at p. 312. As to "rules of court" see 52–3 V. c. 63, s. 14.

[2] See for example s. 15 (1) of the Agriculture Act of 1920 (10–1 G. 5, c. 76) and, as to its operation, footnote (3) to p. 39 below.

[3] Occasionally a rule-making authority makes the same document do duty as draft rules under section 1 and provisional rules under section 2. See the Rules of the Supreme Court (Indemnity Act), 1921, of April 11, 1921.

[4] Afterwards postponed; see footnote at p. 49 below.

"provisional," there is no particular incentive to convert them into non-provisional rules. There are some Provisional Rules of 1911 about Old Age Pensions, reissued in modified form in 1920, but still provisional. And there are Provisional Rules of 1902 and 1904 about Congested Districts in Ireland, of 1911 about Irish Land Purchase and of 1912 about National Insurance procedure in Ireland which still survive in provisional form. Though "provisional" under section 2 of the Rules Publication Act, they have just as much force as if made under section 1. The only difference is that they are not numbered and registered for publication like statutory rules made under section 1. They are issued in similar form.

(4) The fourth point to be insisted upon in delegated legislation is publicity.

Like all other law it ought not only to be certain but also to be ascertainable. We do not want to be shot at dawn to-morrow and not know why. We have just seen that, under section 1 of the Rules Publication Act, notice of intention to make draft rules must be published in the "Gazette," so that the public, in being informed of its ante-natal opportunity to criticise and of the place where copies of the proposed rules can be obtained, is indirectly informed that legislation is impending. As soon as rules have been finally made, they should have as great post-natal publicity as statutes, for they are just as much part of the law which the King's subjects are taken to know. The system of numbering, printing and placing on sale of such rules is governed by section 3 of the Rules Publication Act and by regulations made thereunder. Subject to limitations which will be discussed in a subsequent chapter[1], this system ensures that the public can obtain copies of all delegated legislation.

(5) The fifth and last point is that there should be machinery for amending or revoking delegated legislation as required.

Under the Interpretation Act of 1889[2] if a statute gives power to make rules, regulations or bye-laws, that power—unless the

---

[1] See pp. 45–7 below.
[2] 52–3 V. c. 63, s. 32 (3). Rules and regulations here do not include orders, so that, it seems, the successive Trade Board wages orders cannot specifically repeal the tangle of orders which they supersede.

contrary intention appears—is to be construed as including a power to revoke or vary them. Parliament, of course, can directly amend delegated legislation; it can also do so indirectly by delegating the power to amend. Where the rule-making authority is not a public department, it is not uncommon to insist that its rules should be subject to the approval or confirmation of a department of State or public officer. More than four centuries ago Parliament took notice of the fact that the ordinances of craft fellowships, gilds and fraternities were often unlawful and unreasonable. These minor law-making bodies were forbidden to make statutes without first submitting them for the approval of the Chancellor, Treasurer and Chief Justices of either Bench (or any three of them) or the circuit judges of the shire concerned[1].

The bye-laws of railway companies require the approval of the Minister of Transport, formerly the Board of Trade. The bye-laws of sanitary authorities under the Public Health Act of 1875 were subject to supervision and alteration by the Local Government Board, now the Ministry of Health. Sir Mackenzie Chalmers has preserved some specimens of the legislation which the Local Government Board was thus enabled to avert[2]. They include bye-laws prohibiting boys from throwing stones in the town, prohibiting the singing of hymns in the streets, prohibiting strangers from bringing in dogs and prohibiting "lounging" on Sunday afternoons.

Similarly the universities and colleges of Oxford and Cambridge even if formerly empowered by their royal charters to legislate unrestricted, now have to submit any fresh statute to His Majesty in Council for approval.

This kind of special supervision by some central authority ought to be favourable to a reasonable measure of uniformity Sometimes indeed the object of promoting uniformity is specifically mentioned by Parliament as in the Roads Act and Government of Ireland Act of 1920[3]. Uniformity was the reason given for empowering the Home Secretary in England and the Lord Lieutenant in Ireland to make regulations for the police force

---

[1] 15 H. 6, c. 6: 19 H. 7, c. 7, s. 1.
[2] "Local Government" (Macmillan, 1883), p. 154.
[3] 10–1 G. 5, c. 72, s. 1 (5); 10–1 G. 5, c. 67, ss. 2 (1), 10 (2).

in 1839 and 1836 respectively instead of leaving the matter to local justices as had been the practice on other similar occasions[1].

To add a special safeguard in particular cases, Parliament has invented a device by which it itself supervises delegated legislation. In delegating legislative authority it stipulates that the rules or regulations made thereunder shall be laid before both Houses as soon as made. The rules or regulations take effect forthwith, but, if within a specified number of days either House takes exception to any of them and presents an address on the subject to His Majesty, then the rule or regulation which is objected to may be annulled by Order in Council, though it is usually provided that such annulment shall be without prejudice to the validity of any action already taken under the legislation which is annulled[2].

This post-natal safeguard may, and often does, come upon the top of an ante-natal safeguard, as an example will show. The Dangerous Drugs Act of 1920 gave the Home Secretary power to regulate the production, possession and distribution of raw opium, cocaine and certain other drugs. Section 11 of the Act provides that the regulations when made shall be laid forthwith before each House of Parliament and shall be subject to annulment by Order in Council on address by either House to His Majesty within twenty-one days. These regulations being rules to be laid before Parliament, the ante-natal provisions of section 1 of the Rules Publication Act apply. Accordingly the Home Office notified in the "London Gazette" of January 7th, 1921, the intention to issue regulations and the fact that draft copies of the proposed regulations could be obtained on application to Whitehall. Then followed the period of collecting criticisms and meeting objections. There was, as it happened, some controversy at this stage. Opposition displayed itself by the usual method of newspaper correspondence and questions in Parliament[3]. Finally on May 20th the regulations were made

---

[1] See 2–3 V. c. 93, s. 3 and 6–7 W. 4, c. 13, s. 6, and contrast these with 1–2 W. 4, c. 41, s. 4 and 6–7 W. 4, c. 29, s. 5.
[2] See, for example, 9–10 G. 5, c. 35, s. 7 (3) as to Housing Regulations.
[3] See " The Times " for 1921, Feb. 9, 10 (leading article), 11, March 7 and 10 (article), Hansard, " Commons," vol. 138, pp. 251–6 (see also vol. 143, pp. 774–8), and Report of Committee (Cmd. 1307).

and published as a Statutory Rule and Order, taking effect immediately although for twenty-one sitting days after May 24th (when Parliament next sat) the regulations were liable to be annulled on an address to His Majesty. No such address was presented, so we can assume that the facilities for ante-natal discussion had removed the objections.

Departmentally, it is an obvious advantage of this device of limited post-natal liability to annulment that—unlike "draft" rules laid before Parliament under section 1 of the Rules Publication Act—such rules or regulations are valid from the first moment of their appearance. The disadvantage is that, in thus placing delegated legislation under sentence of death for the first weeks of its life, the successful working of the device depends upon the amount of time which members of Parliament can spare to scrutinise every paper which is laid before the House. An official list is prepared for members which shows the several rules and regulations lying upon the table of the House, the statute under which they are made, and the period for which they are laid; but it would not be uncommon to find as many as sixty sets of rules and regulations in that list at one time.

Evidently this post-natal safeguard makes rule-making authorities careful, for the death sentence is in practice very seldom executed. Article 25 of the Old Age Pensions Regulations of October 1908 was withdrawn in the following December in consequence of an Address presented to His Majesty by the House of Lords[1]; and part of the Housing (Assisted Scheme) Regulations, 1919, was annulled in consequence of an Address presented by the House of Commons[2]. Industry might exhume further examples but they are probably rare[3].

Sometimes, and a little needlessly, the prospect of annulment is made even more remote, for an Act which makes use of this device occasionally omits to specify that the days during which the delegated legislation is to lie before Parliament must be days on which Parliament is sitting. For example, Orders regu-

[1] See "Stat. Rules and Orders," 1908 (No. 1319), p. 712.
[2] See "Stat. Rules and Orders," 1919, No. 2040.
[3] The Lords' address against the Draft Agricultural Improvements Regulations, 1921 (see Hansard, "Debates," May 24, 1921) is a parallel instance under an ante-natal provision (10–1 G. 5, c. 76, s. 15 (1)).

lating the remuneration of solicitors must be laid before Parliament for a month under an Act of 1881. An Order increasing their fees was laid before Parliament on December 11th, 1919. Parliament was very busy finishing up the Session and, after rising for Christmas, did not meet again till February. As the statutory month under the 1881 Act need not be a month during which Parliament is sitting there was a chance for members to overlook the existence of the Order until too late.

This provision for laying rules before the House subject to post-natal annulment is now so common that the time seems almost ripe for co-ordinating and standardising the ante-natal and post-natal procedure and superseding section 1 of the Rules Publication Act, to the operation of which, as we have seen, there are at present certain somewhat arbitrary exceptions. If a fresh Act were passed it might well specify a uniform period during which rules should be subject to annulment. At present that period varies from statute to statute. Sometimes it is 21 days, sometimes twelve weeks, sometimes 100 days and so on. The Act might insist too that the days should be days on which Parliament was sitting. It might also make clear whether Saturdays or other blank days are to be reckoned in the total or not. At present the practice of different Departments is understood to vary. But perhaps absolute uniformity is undesirable. If and when Parliament desires to exercise exceptional supervision, exceptional safeguards can be provided. Under the Emergency Powers Act of 1920, when a state of emergency has been proclaimed, regulations made by Order in Council must be laid before Parliament, but do not operate for more than seven days unless continued by resolution of both Houses[1].

In consulting any document which purports to be a statutory rule or order, the first thing to do is to ascertain (if necessary by reference to the statute under which it is made) whether the rule or order is already valid or whether it is incomplete until some further formality is discharged or some period of time has elapsed. Parliamentary control of delegated legislation through

---

[1] See 10–1 G. 5, c. 55, s. 2. The continuing resolution may amend the regulations thereby continued. See Hansard, "Commons Debates," April 6, May 4 and June 2, 1921.

insistence on the laying of the legislation at some stage or other before both Houses is exercised in fact in such a diversity of circumstances that it is worth while to distinguish the principal varieties[1].

(a) There is the ante-natal laying of draft rules with forty days' notice under section 1 of the Rules Publication Act as already described. In this case the rules while so laid have no effect; they are merely a proposal.

(b) There is the ante-natal laying of draft rules—for example under the Prison Acts—for a certain number of days, with a proviso that on an address being presented by either House no further proceedings shall be taken on the draft. Here again, the rules while so laid have no effect; they are in a state of suspended animation.

(c) Thirdly there is the ante-natal laying of rules in draft with the proviso that they shall not take effect unless positively approved by a resolution of both Houses. This process is applied to certain rules made under the Government of India Act, 1919[2].

(d) Lastly there is the post-natal laying of rules subject to annulment on objection within a specified time, usually twenty-one days[3]. The rules in such a case take effect from the moment of laying.

It may be added that the duty of laying rules and orders before Parliament is not to be evaded by laying them on the table in dummy. An Order of the House of Commons (dated April 13th, 1900) insists that a complete copy of any such document must be laid in order to comply with any statutory condition of this kind[4].

To sum up, insistence upon the safeguards which we have mentioned in this chapter ought to protect us sufficiently against arbitrary or unreasonable legislation by secondary law-making bodies. If Parliament and the public are reasonably vigilant, the safeguards should be adequate. It was never so easy as it is now, to stir public opinion and to focus opposition to an objectionable measure.

[1] See generally the forms given by Ilbert in "Legislative Methods and Forms" at pp. 310–7.   [2] 9–10 G. 5, c. 101, s. 44.
[3] See, for example, the 1919 Housing Act, 9–10 G. 5, c. 35, s. 7 (3).
[4] Ilbert, "Legislative Methods and Forms," p. 311.

CHAPTER V

FORM AND PUBLICATION

STUDENTS of structural form can trace a general improvement in the framing of Acts of Parliament. The conveyancer's influence, tending to long recitals and a non-stop run of the sentences, is disappearing. Bentham gave us the numbered paragraphs and the definition clauses. Short titles are an additional advantage. This improvement in form has naturally spread from the statute book to the secondary legislation of regulations, rules and orders, since the latter are in cases of difficulty drafted in the Parliamentary Counsel's office[1]. The secondary legislation tends to retain the preamble which (except in the case of statutes introducing great constitutional changes) has been discontinued in Acts of Parliament. Statutes no longer recite their object; preambles merely waste time since they multiply the opportunities for discussion and divisions. Acts of Parliament do not need to flaunt their pedigree; their position is assured. On the other hand, statutory rules and orders—which may be judicially challenged—incline to emphasise the statutory authority under which they are made and without which they would have no effect. In other respects—the definition clause, short title, commencement of operation provisions, schedule of repeals and so on—delegated legislation undoubtedly approximates in form to direct legislation. Indeed, the statutory rule and order ought to be more elegant and shapely than the Act of Parliament. When Parliament has passed an Act, the draft Bill carefully constructed by a few experts has often been amended by a multitude of amateurs. Debate in a large assembly and the opportunism of party opposition play havoc with symmetrical draftsmanship unless the Bill deals with technical matters outside the atmosphere of controversy.

The statutory rule and order, being seldom controversial and seldom discussed, may hope to come into operation in the form

[1] See Ilbert, "Legislative Methods and Forms," p. 94. As to the interpretation of regulations etc., see 52–3 V. c. 63, s. 31.

in which its expert designers first fashioned it. Being on the whole of a more temporary character than an Act of Parliament, it is perhaps more likely to be amended from time to time. Where possible, it is certainly an advantage if the amending order can bodily replace and supersede the previous provisions. For this purpose the reprinting clause familiar in the Army Act[1] and in certain other Acts has been usefully introduced into delegated legislation—for example in the Defence of the Realm Regulations, Restoration of Order in Ireland Regulations, Aliens Order, etc. It enables regulations, whenever from time to time reprinted, to be reprinted as a whole with all amendments incorporated. This consolidating device may not always be convenient, but there is something unsatisfactory about the alternative as can be seen on an inspection of the existing warrants about postage rates. The Inland Post Warrant of 1903 has been amended twenty-two times, the Foreign and Colonial Parcel Post Warrant of 1906 no fewer than ninety-nine times. This is making delegated legislation as complicated in form as the statute book itself. The Benthamite idea that law should be contained in a single code simple enough for the layman to understand has even greater force in the case of delegated legislation than in the case of the statute book, because the statute book is perhaps more often consulted by lawyers than by laymen, whereas the delegated legislation is probably more often consulted by laymen than by lawyers. Rules and regulations therefore, should be fool-proof. If one rule repeals another, it should do so specifically. The department which issues it knows what effect it has upon previous rules, and ought not to keep that knowledge to itself[2]. Here is a minor instance of making the riddle harder. A set of regulations in 1920 contained this clause: "The provisions of the...Regulations, 1914, and the corresponding Regulations applicable to Scotland, Ireland and Wales, shall so far as inconsistent with these Regulations, cease to have effect." Our administration is partly in the hands of laymen and we do not want to drive laymen out of public life. But such a clause is asking a layman to attempt feats of legal interpretation and

---

[1] Introduced for the purpose of the periodical reprinting of the Army Act by 48–9 V. c. 8, s. 8 (2).   [2] But see footnote 2 to p. 36 above.

construction and to hunt for virtual repeals; in addition, if he is a Scot, an Irishman or a Welshman, he has to examine the English regulations in order to find out which of his own regulations correspond thereto. Departments possess this kind of information and might as well furnish it.

The documentary form in which statutory rules and orders are officially published is governed by section 3 of the Rules Publication Act and by the Treasury regulations made thereunder[1]. Before that Act was passed, delegated legislation was almost undiscoverable. Part of it was buried in the pages of the "London Gazette," the arid nature of which still justifies Macaulay's criticisms; the rest was scattered over Parliamentary Papers or other departmental documents or files without any definite system.

Since 1893 statutory rules and orders have been printed on a methodical plan under the editorship of Mr Alexander Pulling[2]. Each one is headed with a main serial number year by year. The legal orders and the Scottish orders also have a subsidiary serial number preceded by the letters L. and S. respectively[3]. All are classified and labelled under their general heading of law and are usually prefaced with a brief summary stating by whom they are made, at what date, and under what Act of Parliament. As the documents are printed in uniform octavo size and thus placed on sale, it has ceased to be necessary to print them also in the different type and setting of the "Gazette." The Rules Publication Act provides that where any statute requires rules to be published in the "Gazette," it shall in future be sufficient merely to notify in the "Gazette" the fact that the rules have been made and the place where copies can be purchased. Statutory Rules and Orders are admissible in evidence in legal proceedings by virtue of the Documentary Evidence Act[4].

---

[1] The Act and the Treasury Regulations are printed for convenient reference in Appendix I at p. 57 below. Orders (see footnote 3 to p. 33 above) may be "statutory rules" within the meaning of section 3. See subsection (4) at p. 58 and reg. 2 at p. 59 below.

[2] For a list of the official publications relating to Statutory Rules and Orders, see Appendix II at p. 61 below.

[3] See the heading to the Scottish Order printed as an illustration at p. 67 below.

[4] 31–2 V. c. 37, s. 2, as extended to various departments and ministries (see the third column opposite this statute in vol. I of the official Chronological

The creation of this official system of publication has removed the reproach that the law embodied in statutory rules was less well known and less easy to find than the law embodied in Acts of Parliament. Nevertheless the title Statutory Rules and Orders is not synonymous with delegated legislation, for the official system of publication does not cover the whole field. The system, as has been stated, is based on section 3 of the Act of 1893, and section 3 was a kind of afterthought introduced in the later stages of a Bill originally designed to apply only to rules about legal procedure. The Act therefore, even when finally extended to other rules, was not dealing with all delegated legislation but with the legislation made by certain "rule-making authorities." "Rule-making authority" was defined by section 4 as including "every authority authorised to make any statutory rules." "Statutory rules" were defined as meaning

rules, regulations or bye-laws made under any Act of Parliament which,

(*a*) relate to any court in the United Kingdom or to the procedure, practice, costs or fees therein, or to any fees or matters applying generally throughout England, Scotland or Ireland; or

(*b*) are made by Her Majesty in Council, the Judicial Committee, the Treasury, the Lord Chancellor of Great Britain or the Lord Lieutenant or Lord Chancellor of Ireland, or a Secretary of State, the Admiralty, the Board of Trade, the Local Government Board for England or Ireland, the Chief Secretary for Ireland, or any other Government Department.

Many of the bodies to which Parliament has delegated legislative power are excluded by this definition. A railway is not a "rule-making" authority nor is a municipal corporation; their bye-laws are therefore not statutory rules and orders.

There are other classes of secondary legislation which also escape the net of section 3 of the Rules Publication Act.

A large number are ruled out because they are merely confirmatory[1], others because they are of an executive rather than a legislative character. This latter distinction corresponds roughly with the distinction between general and particular

Table and Index to the Statutes in Force). See also 45–6 V.c.9, s.2 as to documents published under authority, and 8–9 V.c.113, s.1 as to proof of bye-laws.

[1] For example the statutes of colleges at Oxford and Cambridge which are merely confirmed by a rule-making authority (see 40–1 V. c. 48, s. 49).

commands which various writers have discussed. It approximately follows Blackstone's statement that legislation is a rule, not a transient sudden order from a superior to or concerning a particular person but something permanent, uniform and universal[1]. Confidential rules are also excluded; so also, subject to the direction of the Treasury with the approval of the Lord Chancellor and Speaker, are annual or periodically renewed rules such as the militia regulations or the education codes. The editor is allowed a discretion; if doubts arise, questions are decided by the Treasury, Lord Chancellor and Speaker.

Not every document which is officially registered and numbered is printed. Many which are of local interest are not printed, but are tabulated in a classified list at the end of the annual volumes of Statutory Rules and Orders. If departments think it unnecessary to have their orders printed, their wishes are considered. And not every Statutory Rule and Order is put on sale. Sometimes the department makes a free distribution to the persons concerned.

Finally Statutory Rules and Orders have been interpreted as being only those which are descended immediately from Acts of Parliament. If a rule or order is made by virtue of a previous rule or order, then the result is not the child but the grand-child of an Act of Parliament; it is not statutory but sub-statutory, and therefore it has strictly no right to be published in the series[2]. This distinction between child and grand-child did not greatly matter until August, 1914, but during the war the Defence of the Realm Act had numbers of grand-children: the Defence of the Realm Regulations were the immediate parents, the Act was the grand-parent. Mr Alexander Pulling came to the rescue by producing a set of manuals of emergency legislation which introduced these grand-children to the public.

---

[1] See Pollock, "First Book of Jurisprudence," p. 35. The distinction for the purpose of publication or non-publication in the official series is best illustrated by the orders issued under s. 3 of the Naval and Marine Pay and Pensions Act of 1865. A new rate of naval pay throughout the service would undoubtedly be treated as legislative rather than executive, but not a new "colonial allowance" for the officer in charge of defensive arming of merchant ships at Dakar in 1918.

[2] See the Order printed as an illustration at p. 67 below; in this case the editor has in his discretion disregarded the distinction.

From what has been said, it also follows that the official series does not include orders made by virtue of the prerogative instead of by virtue of an Act of Parliament. These prerogative orders, which deal with such matters as the constitution and currency of parts of the Empire overseas, are however gathered up by the Editor of the annual volumes of Statutory Rules and Orders and printed by him in an Appendix thereto.

If ever the Rules Publication Act were amended or replaced, opportunity would no doubt be taken to review the scope of section 3. The distinction between statutory and sub-statutory rules and regulations is too artificial to bear explanation to the public which is concerned to know what laws it must obey. Amongst other forms of delegated legislation which require publication in some form, but which fall outside the section, are the "measures" of the Church of England National Assembly. These receive royal assent and have the force of Acts of Parliament, but are neither Acts nor statutory rules and orders. They are another form of indirect or informal Parliamentary legislation, being recommended for royal assent on a resolution of both Houses of Parliament. The resolutions of Parliament sometimes have legislative effect; for example they could reduce the hours of work underground in collieries from seven hours to six under the Coal Mines Act of 1919, and they can amend regulations under the Emergency Powers Act of 1920. Not being formal Acts of Parliament, the resolutions of Parliament do not appear in the statute book, and, Parliament not being a "rule-making authority," they are not statutory rules and orders. There should be some recognised uniform system of publishing all secondary legislation of this kind which is of public importance.

CHAPTER VI

HISTORICAL DEVELOPMENT

WE cannot flatter our national self-esteem by claiming a monopoly in so valuable an administrative and legislative weapon as the statutory rule and order system provides. Other countries, and notably France and Italy, have delegated legislative power far more freely[1]. But we can claim that we have managed to make the greatest possible use of that weapon consistent with the supremacy of Parliament. Indeed each successive delegation of legislative power has been a fresh recognition of that supremacy.

The powers which the executive exercises without Parliamentary authority are comprised under the comprehensive term "prerogative." Where Parliament has intervened and has provided by statute for powers previously within the prerogative being exercised in a particular manner and subject to the limitations contained in statute, they can only be so exercised. Otherwise what use would there be in imposing limitations if the Crown could at its pleasure disregard them and fall back on the prerogative[2]?

The Crown being a party to every Act of Parliament, it is logical to assume that the Crown assents to the prerogative being to that extent curtailed[3]. The successive delegations by Parliament, therefore, are victories at the expense of the Crown. The executive nowadays would hesitate before invoking the prerogative to effect something which Parliament had declined to sanction[4]. The expansion of the field of delegated legislation is going on under our eyes all the while. The Act passed to regulate the 1911 census was careful to specify the date of the

---

[1] See Ilbert, "Legislative Methods and Forms," pp. 38-9.
[2] Per Swinfen Eady M.R., *A.-G.* v. *De Keyser's Hotel* [1919] 2 Ch. at p. 216, cited [1920] A.C. at p. 526. This case is best studied in "The Case of Requisition" (Oxford Press, 1920).
[3] See Lord Dunedin, *A.-G.* v. *De Keyser's Hotel* [1920] A.C. at p. 526.
[4] For the famous case in which Gladstone abolished by royal warrant the purchase of military commissions, see Morley, "Gladstone," II, pp. 361-5; Buckle, "Disraeli," V, p. 141.

census and the exact details (name, sex, age, occupation, birth-place, etc.) to be entered upon the census form. In the new and permanent Census Act of 1920 these points are left to be dealt with by Order in Council and the details of information required may include any matters "with respect to which it is desirable to obtain statistical information with a view to ascertaining the social or civil condition of the population[1]." Thus delegation increases in a decade.

A casual glance through the statutes of 1919 and 1920 shows that rather more than half the Acts of those years delegated legislative power of some kind or other—roughly 60 out of 102 Acts in 1919 and 47 out of 82 Acts in 1920. A hundred years ago we were not yet departmentalised. The Defence Acts passed to protect us against Napoleon never contemplated the issue of Defence of the Realm Regulations. If we go back a century to the years 1819 and 1820, we find plenty of talk of "regulations" in Acts of Parliament, but they are regulations actually contained in the Acts not regulations to be made by some other authority. Thus in the factory and workshop legislation of a century ago the ages of employees in cotton mills are specified; the hours of work are fixed; there is a definite time for breakfast and a definite time for dinner[2]. There is no margin for elasticity; nothing is left to be arranged by departmental order; we were not yet so elaborately administered. The Acts of the period are full of almost grotesque detail for want of the practice of entrusting minor matters to subordinate legislation. Nevertheless, there were examples even then, of delegation. The British Herring Fisheries Commissioners could make regulations about payment of bounty, shipment of salt and exportation of fish[3]—such matters as the Ministry of Agriculture and Fisheries would deal with to-day. The Commissioners of Irish Fisheries could also make regulations[4], though the regulations they could make

---

[1] See 10–1 G. 5, c. 41, s. 1. The Act illustrates the administrative convenience of delegation: the date of the census was fixed by Order as April 24th, 1921, but was postponed in view of the industrial crisis. The 1911 date having been fixed by statute an amending Act would have been necessary for a postponement.

[2] See 60 G. 3, c. 66. Compare 42 G. 3, c. 73.

[3] 1 G. 4, c. 103, s. 6.   [4] 1 G. 4, c. 82, s. 21.

are trifling compared with the detailed regulations already contained in the Act. The Irish Court of Exchequer could vary its table of fees by order of Court[1]. The Lord Lieutenant could reduce the statutory rate of interest on public works loans in Ireland[2]. There is a hint that the Treasury can make rules as to the drawing of lotteries[3]. Otherwise there is not much delegation in those two years[4]. Perhaps the only example of a statutory Order in Council is in the Act authorising justices to seize arms in certain disturbed counties; there is power to make proclamations extending the Act to other counties or withdrawing its operation in the counties prescribed[5]. At this stage, the practice of delegating legislative power is already understood, but Parliament is still able to do by itself almost all the legislating that the country requires.

If we cannot name the earliest instance of delegation, we can at least say which was the most striking of early instances. It is the Statute of Proclamations passed in 1539, the "Act that Proclamations made by the King shall be obeyed[6]." The main provision of this *lex regia* was that which empowered Henry VIII with the advice of a majority of his Council, to set forth proclamations under such penalties and pains and of such sort as to His Majesty and his said council should seem necessary and requisite, the said proclamations to be obeyed, observed and kept as though they were made by Act of Parliament unless the King's Highness dispense with any of them under his great seal. In addition to various sections as to the penalties and procedure under the Act, there is a clause which prescribes that every sheriff or other officer to whom His Majesty's proclamations are directed, shall, within fourteen days proclaim them in market-towns, other towns or villages and post them up "openly upon places convenient" therein. Here then are all the elements of a delegation of legislative power by Parliament and the elements of a Rules Publication Act as well. And, as a second example of delegated legislation from the same reign, three or four years later there was another Act of Parliament—

---

[1] 1 G. 4, c. 68, s. 2.
[2] 1 G. 4, c. 81, s. 4.
[3] 1 G. 4, c. 72, s. 3.
[4] See 1 G. 4, c. 39, ss. 9, 39.
[5] 60 G. 3, c. 2, ss. 8, 9.
[6] 31 H. 8, c. 8.

of less notoriety and of narrower application, yet equally significant for our purpose—which empowered the King to alter the laws of Wales and to make laws and ordinances for Wales, such alterations and new laws and ordinances to be published under the great seal and to be of as good strength, virtue and effect as if made by the authority of Parliament[1].

This latter Act remained on the statute book for nearly a century[2]. The Statute of Proclamations was repealed as soon as Henry died[3]. Those eight years during which the *Lex regia* was in force might be considered the golden age of delegated legislation. A self-effacing Parliament had given the Crown such unfettered powers of independent legislation as have never been conceded since. But though the text-books dilate upon this singular enactment, they often convey a false impression. From their comments we might suppose that in 1539 Parliament servilely abandoned its functions and ceased to exercise them whilst Henry had the design, the opportunity and the power of proposing and enforcing measures as he pleased. It is not so. Parliament was not entirely subservient; it met and worked just as hard after 1539 as before; it opposed several of the Bills proposed by the King, and even threw some out altogether. Henry, on his side continued to use Parliament as part of the legislative machinery of the country, nor are the proclamations which he issued after 1539 more autocratic than those which he had issued before. Roughly a quarter of them are merely the publication or exposition of statutes. The remaining three-quarters are concerned with such matters as coinage, prices, victualling, wines, kersies, heretical books, vagabonds, aliens, war and peace with France and so on[4]; they indicate no variation of pre-1539 legislative conditions[5].

The simplest explanation of the Act of Proclamations is to accept the two reasons set forth in the preamble. The Act recites firstly that certain recent proclamations by the King

[1] 34–5 H. 8, c. 26, s. 59.   [2] See 21 J. 1, c. 10.
[3] See 1 E. 6, c. 12, s. 5.
[4] See the catalogue of Tudor and Stuart Proclamations (edited by Mr Steele) in the "Bibliotheca Lindesiana."
[5] This is the view taken by Professor A. F. Pollard, in the "Evolution of Parliament," pp. 266–8.

(particularly on religious matters) had been contemned, and it was necessary to define the power to punish such disobedience. Secondly it recites the reasonable political opinion (which we have already discussed[1]) that "sudden occasions" may arise when there is no time to "abide for a Parliament" and when some "speedy remedy" is essential. His Majesty "by the kingly and royal power given him by God may do many things in such cases" but should not be "driven to extend the liberty and supremacy of his royal power and dignity by wilfulness of froward subjects."

Here then we see Parliament beginning to use its now familiar device of limiting the prerogative while conferring statutory powers upon the Crown. The Act of Proclamations looks like the concession to the Crown by Parliament of unlimited legislative authority. Yet it can also be looked upon as a surrender by the Crown of the old unlimited prerogative power. Henceforward if Henry wanted to make law by a proclamation he had to take account of the constitutional doctrine recited in the preamble and to exercise his powers subject to any limitation the Act might contain. He had admitted that it was for Parliament to permit him to legislate. In this sense the Act was as much a triumph for Parliament as for the Crown. Possibly it was one of those English compromises where both sides can feel they have obtained advantage. The Bill as Henry first set it before Parliament was far more Henrican than the Act as it was eventually passed[2]. If the Act is represented merely as a triumph for Parliament, we have to explain why it was so promptly repealed as soon as Henry was dead. The repealing Act of Edward VI was an "Act for the repeal of certain statutes concerning treasons and felonies." Henry had invented far too many new treasons and the Act of Proclamations contained one of them, it being treason to disobey the Act and depart the Realm to escape the consequences. Perhaps it was mainly because it was a treason-making Act that the great *lex regia* was repealed.

The Act of 1539 is a high-water mark in delegated legislation.

[1] See pp. 21–6 above.
[2] See Professor A. F. Pollard, "Henry VIII," p. 264.

Thereafter the tide recedes. Elizabeth and James are reactionary; they rely on the prerogative. Rulers by divine right disdain to be the delegates of Parliament. Parliament had to re-assert its power over legislation, to define the prerogative and thus to prepare the way for delegation in the future. By steps too well known to require recapitulation, by presentment of grievance, by remonstrance and by vindication of common law, Parliament was to win and consolidate its position. What it had to contend against may be illustrated by this extract from the Petition for redress of Grievances, presented in 1610:

It is apparent both that proclamations have been of late years much more frequent than heretofore, and that they are extended not only to the liberties but also to the goods, inheritances and livelihood of men, some of them tending to alter some points of the law, and make them new, other some made shortly after a Session of Parliament for matter directly rejected in the same Session...some containing penalties in form of penal statutes...and some vouching former proclamations to countenance and warrant the latter...by reason whereof there is a general fear conceived and spread amongst your Majesty's people that proclamations will by degrees grow up and increase to the strength and nature of laws[1].

One famous battle in the long constitutional campaign was fought over the power to tax overseas trade. The Crown claimed the right to act under the prerogative, and Parliament had from time to time either actually delegated power to the Crown or had passed Acts which saved and admitted the prerogative. Thus Henry VIII was given statutory authority to make proclamations for the repeal or subsequent revival of Acts made during a particular Parliament for restraint of imports or exports[2], and Parliament expressly recognised the right both of Elizabeth and of James to prohibit the export of corn[3]. Under the prerogative Mary and Elizabeth imposed duties on wine, and James brought the matter to a head by imposing a duty on currants in addition to the duty which Parliament had already imposed. Bates refused to pay. The Court of Exchequer decided that James was right and Bates was wrong. Coke has given us

---

[1] S.P. Dom. Jac. I, LVI, 10.   [2] 26 H. 8, c. 10.
[3] See 13 Eliz. c. 13, ss. 1, 4; 35 Eliz. c. 7, s. 14; 1 J. 1, c. 25, s. 3; 21 J. 1, c. 28, s. 4, etc.

to understand that he did not quite agree with the Barons of the Exchequer, yet even he admits that as a matter of policy, to advance trade and traffic, *pro bono publico*, the prerogative might be justified[1].

These controversies are worth mentioning as stages by which Parliament was led to assert itself. Coke's view of the proclamations of James I in another famous case is on record. Could the King legislate by proclamation to prohibit new buildings in and about London? Could he similarly prohibit the making of starch out of wheat? Coke was not the man to exalt the prerogative over the common law.

The King by his proclamation cannot create any offence which was not an offence before, for then he may alter the law of the land by his proclamation in a high point.... The King hath no prerogative but that which the law of the land allows him. But the King for prevention of offences may by proclamation admonish his subjects that they keep the laws and do not offend them[2]....

Though the common law had thus been vindicated, the prerogative lived on in a kind of silver age, issuing proclamations nevertheless till the end of the Stuart dynasty. The proclamation, it is true, is not solely employed for legislation. It may be used for executive rather than legislative purposes, or for some purpose on the border line between the two. The constitutional struggle raged as fiercely over the one kind as the other; there were penal consequences in either case, and, so long as the Star Chamber existed, there was a tribunal which would enforce them.

When Parliament had won its battles and attained to "constitutional monarchy," the struggle gradually ceased to be one between Parliament and the Crown. And when Parliament began to realise the convenience and even the necessity for delegating legislative power, it was easy to make use of the old machinery and to permit the statutory Order in Council to do

---

[1] Co. Rep. xii, 238. To-day not the Crown but the department incurs political odium. See, for example, Hansard "Commons Debates" (Safeguarding of Industries Bill), June 6, 1921, pp. 1594–5.

[2] Case of Proclamations, Co. Rep. xii, 74. Possibly we owe to this opinion the principle (see Ilbert, "Legislative Methods and Forms," p. 310) that delegated legislation should not authorise the imposition of penalties except such penalties as are usually attached to the breach of bye-laws.

what the prerogative Order in Council had been restrained from doing[1]. The statutory Order in Council is the most important form of delegated legislation. Until our administrative departments (which in some instances are off-shoots of the Privy Council) reached their present elaboration, the King in Council or the Privy Council was the obvious authority available to undertake to make rules and regulations. The more elaborate our departments become, the more do they take over the legislative powers entrusted in time past by Parliament to the Privy Council. Yet, even now, though the Home Office is specially concerned with aliens and the Air Council with aerial navigation, the big codes governing those topics are issued not on the authority of the heads of those departments but on the authority of an Order in Council. Doubtless the department prepares the drafts, but the formal legislative act is made more dignified —one might almost say more national—by being united with the traditions of the King in Council.

At present there are signs of a reaction from that process of multiplying departments and departmental regulations which was developed by the special conditions of a great war. If liberty is felt to be imperilled, it is no longer the Crown which can be attacked, for the Crown no longer runs counter to the wishes of Parliament. It is the department which is regarded as the enemy. It is the department which has been heard to justify its actions by pleading the prerogative in a tone which has not been used since Stuart times.

But the war is over and we can see things in perspective again.

The idea that the King in Council, or indeed any branch of the executive, has power to prescribe or alter the law to be administered by Courts of law in this country, is out of harmony with the principles of our constitution. It is true that, under a number of modern statutes, various branches of the executive have power to make rules having the force of statutes, but all such rules derive their validity from the statute which creates the power and not from the executive body by which they are made[2].

---

[1] Statutory Orders are naturally elaborated both in form and in purpose beyond the compass of prerogative Orders. "There is no prerogative to make regulations" observed Lord Sumner in *Att.-Gen.* v. *De Keyser's Hotel* [1920] A.C. at p. 557.

[2] Per Lord Parker, *The Zamora* (1916), A.C. at p. 90.

These words of Lord Parker emphasise once more the fact that delegated legislation descends directly from Acts of Parliament. Parliament would not delegate legislative power to administrative departments unless those departments asked for it. If that power were abused, Parliament would hesitate to grant it when it is asked for. Our great departments of State know, therefore, that the continued acceptability of this invaluable administrative device depends upon its reasonable use and application.

When in 1911 Lord Cozens-Hardy said that the real legislation was not to be found in the statute-book alone, he frankly described the development of departmental activity as a very bad system and one attended by very great danger[1]. Had he lived to speak in 1921, he would doubtless have repeated his warning, though he might have agreed with Lord Justice Scrutton that war cannot be carried on according to the principles of Magna Carta[2]. The problem is to obtain a form of government which, in Abraham Lincoln's words, is "not too strong for the liberties of its people" and yet "strong enough to maintain its existence in great emergencies."

[1] See "The Times," May 4, 1911, at p. 10.
[2] In *Ronnfeldt* v. *Phillips* (1918), 35 T.L.R. at p. 47.

APPENDIX I

RULES PUBLICATION ACT, 1893, AND TREASURY REGULATIONS MADE THEREUNDER

The Rules Publication Act, 1893 (56–7 V. c. 66).

An Act for the Publication of Statutory Rules.

[21st December 1893.]

BE it enacted by the Queen's most Excellent Majesty, by and with the advice and consent of the Lords Spiritual and Temporal, and Commons, in this present Parliament assembled, and by the authority of the same, as follows:

1.—(1) At least forty days before making any statutory rules to which this section applies, notice of the proposal to make the rules, and of the place where copies of the draft rules may be obtained, shall be published in the London Gazette.

(2) During those forty days any public body may obtain copies of such draft rules on payment of not exceeding threepence per folio, and any representations or suggestions made in writing by a public body interested to the authority proposing to make the rules shall be taken into consideration by that authority before finally settling the rules; and on the expiration of those forty days the rules may be made by the rule-making authority, either as originally drawn or as amended by such authority, and shall come into operation forthwith or at such time as may be prescribed in the rules.

(3) Any enactment which provides that any statutory rules to which this section applies shall not come into operation for a specified period after they are made is hereby repealed, but this repeal shall not affect section thirty-seven of the Interpretation Act, 1889.

(4) The statutory rules to which this section applies are those made in pursuance of any Act of Parliament which directs the statutory rules to be laid before Parliament, but do not include any statutory rules if the same or a draft thereof are required to be laid before Parliament for any period before the rules come into operation, nor do they include rules made by the Local Government Board for England or Ireland, the Board of Trade, or the Revenue Departments or by or for the purposes of the Post Office; nor rules made by the Board of Agriculture under the Contagious Diseases (Animals) Act, 1878, and the Acts amending the same.

(5) This section shall not apply to Scotland.

(6) In the case of any rules which it is proposed shall extend to Ireland, publication in the Dublin Gazette of the notice required by this section shall be requisite in addition to, or, if they extend to Ireland only, in lieu of, publication in the London Gazette.

2. Where a rule-making authority certifies that on account of urgency or any special reason any rule should come into immediate operation, it shall be lawful for such authority to make any such rules to come into operation forthwith as provisional rules, but such provisional rules shall only continue in force until rules have been made in accordance with the foregoing provisions of this Act.

3.—(1) All statutory rules made after the thirty-first day of December next after the passing of this Act shall forthwith after they are made be sent to the Queen's printer of Acts of Parliament, and shall, in accordance with regulations made by the Treasury, with the concurrence of the Lord Chancellor and the Speaker of the House of Commons, be numbered, and (save as provided by the regulations) printed, and sold by him.

(2) Any statutory rules may, without prejudice to any other mode of citation, be cited by the number so given as above mentioned and the calendar year.

(3) Where any statutory rules are required by any Act to be published or notified in the London, Edinburgh, or Dublin Gazette, a notice in the Gazette of the rules having been made, and of the place where copies of them can be purchased, shall be sufficient compliance with the said requirement.

(4) Regulations under this section may provide for the different treatment of statutory rules which are of the nature of public Acts, and of those which are of the nature of local and personal or private Acts; and may determine the classes of cases in which the exercise of a statutory power by any rule-making authority constitutes or does not constitute the making of a statutory rule within the meaning of this section, and may provide for the exemption from this section of any such classes.

(5) In the making of such regulations, each Government department concerned shall be consulted, and due regard had to the views of that department.

4. In this Act—

" Statutory rules " means rules, regulations, or byelaws made under any Act of Parliament which (a) relate to any court in the United Kingdom, or to the procedure, practice, costs, or fees therein, or to any fees or matters applying generally throughout England, Scotland, or Ireland; or (*b*) are made by Her Majesty in Council, the Judicial Committee, the Treasury, the Lord Chancellor of Great Britain, or the Lord Lieutenant or the Lord Chancellor of Ireland, or a Secretary of State, the Admiralty, the Board of Trade, the Local Government Board for England or Ireland, the Chief Secretary for Ireland, or any other Government Department.

"Rule-making authority" includes every authority authorised to make any statutory rules.

5. This Act may be cited as the Rules Publication Act, 1893.

REGULATIONS, DATED AUGUST 9, 1894, MADE BY THE TREASURY WITH THE CONCURRENCE OF THE LORD CHANCELLOR AND THE SPEAKER OF THE HOUSE OF COMMONS IN PURSUANCE OF THE RULES PUBLICATION ACT, 1893

1894. No. 734

Whereas by the Rules Publication Act, 1893, herein-after referred to as "the Act," regulations are authorised to be made by the Treasury, with the concurrence of the Lord Chancellor and the Speaker of the House of Commons, for such purposes in relation to Statutory Rules as are therein mentioned:

Now, therefore, We, the Lords Commissioners of Her Majesty's Treasury, in pursuance of the said Act, and of all other powers in that behalf, do hereby, with the concurrence of the Lord Chancellor and of the Speaker of the House of Commons, make the following regulations:

1. Every exercise of a statutory power by a rule-making authority, which is of a legislative and not an executive character, shall be held to be a Statutory Rule within section three of the Act and these regulations.

2. An exercise of a statutory power which is confirmed only by a rule-making authority shall not be held to be a Statutory Rule within section three of the Act or these regulations.

3. Except as mentioned in Regulation 2, the volumes of Statutory Rules and Orders published by the Stationery Office in 1890, 1891, and 1892 shall form a practical guide for determining those exercises of statutory powers which should be treated as Statutory Rules within section three of the Act and these regulations.

4. A distinction shall be drawn between Statutory Rules which are general and those which are local and personal.

5. The distinction shall follow, unless in exceptional circumstances, that adopted between public Acts and local and personal Acts of Parliament.

6. All Statutory Rules when sent to the Queen's Printer of Acts of Parliament, as required by the Act, shall be numbered consecutively as nearly as may be in the order in which they are received by the Queen's Printer, and either with or without a second number for a particular class of Rules[1].

7. The main series of numbers shall be a separate series for each calendar year, but Statutory Rules made in December in any year, and received by the Queen's Printer of Acts of Parliament within 14 days after the end of that year, may be numbered with the Statutory Rules of that year and included in the annual volume of that year.

8. All Statutory Rules shall be printed and sold unless, in the case of Rules not required to be published in any Gazette, the rule-making authority declare that it is unnecessary to print and sell them, and such declaration is not overruled on a reference under Regulation 15.

9. Statutory Rules similar to public general Acts shall be printed in an annual volume, and that volume shall include a list of the Statutory Rules which are similar to local and personal Acts[2].

10. The rule-making authority, in sending any Statutory Rule to the Queen's Printer of Acts of Parliament, shall state whether they consider the Rule to be general or local and personal, and that statement shall be followed unless overruled on a reference under Regulation 15.

11. In the annual volume of Statutory Rules the general Rules shall be published in a classified form, as in the volumes mentioned above in Regulation 3 which have been hitherto published.

12. Regulations 6 and 8 shall apply to temporary Statutory Rules, but if they have ceased to be in force at the time of the publication of the annual volume, or will so cease a short time afterwards, they shall not be included in that volume, unless the rule-making authority inform the Queen's Printer of Acts of Parliament that they desire them to be so included.

13. The Treasury with the concurrence of the Lord Chancellor and the Speaker of the House of Commons, may direct the exclusion from publication at length in any annual volume, of any Rules which it seems to them unnecessary so to publish by reason of their annual or other periodical renewal; as for instance, the militia regulations, the volunteer regulations, or the education code.

---

[1] Statutory Rules prescribing the Procedure or Fees in any Court in England bear a second number prefaced by the letter " L " (i.e. legal series).

[2] The Classified List at the end of each annual volume corresponds in arrangement to the Classified List of Local Acts in the annual volume of the Statutes.

14. Any Statutory Rule or class of Statutory Rules which, on the application of the rule-making authority, may be determined by the Treasury, with the concurrence of the Lord Chancellor and the Speaker of the House of Commons, to be confidential, shall be exempted from section three of the Act and from these regulations.

15. Any question which arises under Regulation 8 as to the printing and sale of Statutory Rules, or under Regulation 10 as to Statutory Rules being general or local and personal, or which arises on the application or interpretation of these regulations, shall be referred to the Treasury, and determined by them with the concurrence of the Lord Chancellor and the Speaker of the House of Commons.

R. K. CAUSTON,
W. MCARTHUR,
(Commissioners of Her Majesty's Treasury).

I concur,
HERSCHELL, C.

I concur,
ARTHUR W. PEEL,
Speaker.

9th August, 1894.

APPENDIX II

LIST OF OFFICIAL PUBLICATIONS RELATING TO STATUTORY RULES AND ORDERS

1. STATUTORY RULES AND ORDERS issued singly and placed on sale (at prices from a penny upwards) as explained at p. 44 above. Lists of these in serial order are periodically published by the Stationery Office. "Provisional" Rules and Orders (as to which see p. 35 above) are similarly issued and placed on sale.

2. ANNUAL VOLUMES of the STATUTORY RULES AND ORDERS (other than those of a local, personal or temporary character) in force on December 31st of each year. These volumes also contain tables showing (i) the temporary orders which have come into force and expired during the year; (ii) the effect of the year's Rules and Orders upon (a) the statute book and (b) the Statutory Rules and Orders previously in force, as well as (iii) a classified list of the local Orders of the year.

3. STATUTORY RULES AND ORDERS IN FORCE ON DECEMBER 31, 1919. This publication is usually issued once in three years. It shows the statutory powers delegated by the various Acts of Parliament and the exercise of those powers. The contents of the successive Annual Volumes rapidly become obsolete. This publication, being a catalogue of only those orders, &c., which survive at the date of its issue, obviates the labour of searching through those previous volumes.

4. STATUTORY RULES AND ORDERS REVISED, being the Statutory Rules and Orders (other than those of a local, personal or temporary character) in force on December 31st, 1903.

This collective edition in 13 volumes was issued in 1904. A previous collection had been published in 8 volumes in 1890. The several sections which make up the 1904 edition were printed separately, with a view to assisting purchasers to obtain the law on a particular subject without buying the whole 13 volumes.

APPENDIX III

SPECIMEN RULES AND ORDERS

[The following five Orders are printed here to illustrate the form and functions of delegated legislation. In form these specimens correspond to the copies as officially issued except for minor differences of type and except for the omission of the imprint ("Printed and published by His Majesty's Stationery Office"), the notification of price (a penny in each case) and the list of addresses where the Order can be bought. The uniform system of headings (serial number, subject and description) will be noticed. Short Orders have been selected for reasons of space.

The specimens (two Orders in Council, two Board of Trade Orders and one Scottish Office Order) include examples of the "appointed day" procedure, the departmental extension of the scope of an Act (the now defunct Profiteering Act), and the variation of the schedule of an Act. The Scottish Order as to explosives belongs to the class described at p. 46 above as "sub-statutory," since it is authorised not by an Act but by a Regulation made under an Act.]

STATUTORY RULES AND ORDERS,
1919, No. 850.

HEALTH, MINISTRY OF.

THE MINISTRY OF HEALTH ACT, 1919 (DATE OF COMMENCEMENT)
ORDER, 1919.

At the Court at Buckingham Palace, the 25th day of June, 1919.

PRESENT,

The King's Most Excellent Majesty in Council.

Whereas by sub-section (1) of Section 11 of the Ministry of
Health Act, 1919, it is enacted that the Act shall come into operation
upon such day or days as may be appointed by Order in Council
and that different days may be appointed for different purposes and
provisions of the Act.

Now, therefore, His Majesty, by and with the advice of His Privy
Council, in pursuance of the Ministry of Health Act, 1919, and of
all other powers enabling Him in that behalf, is pleased to order, and
it is hereby ordered, as follows:

1. For such of the provisions of the said Act as are hereinafter
mentioned the appointed day shall be—

(1) in the case of Section 1, the 25th day of June, 1919;

(2) in the case of Section 2; paragraphs (*a*), (*b*) and (*e*) and
Proviso (ii) of sub-section (1) and sub-sections (2), (3), (4)
and (5) of Section 3; Sections 4, 5, 6, 7, 8, 9, and 10 and
sub-sections (3) and (4) of Section 11, the 1st day of July,
1919, except so far as paragraph (*a*) of sub-section (1) of
Section 3 relates to powers and duties conferred or imposed
upon the Local Government Board by any Act of Parliament
passed, or Provisional Order confirmed, or other Instrument
made, on or after the 1st day of July, 1919, but during the
present session of Parliament, in respect of which powers
and duties the appointed day shall be the day on which such
Act, Order, or Instrument comes into operation.

2. The Interpretation Act, 1889, applies for the purpose of the
interpretation of this Order as it applies for the interpretation of an
Act of Parliament.

3. This Order may be cited as the Ministry of Health Act, 1919
(Date of Commencement) Order, 1919.

ALMERIC FITZROY.

STATUTORY RULES AND ORDERS,

1920, No. 1443.

PROFITEERING.

THE PROFITEERING ACTS, 1919 AND 1920, ORDER (NO. 9), DATED AUGUST 2, 1920, MADE BY THE BOARD OF TRADE UNDER SECTION 2 OF THE PROFITEERING (AMENDMENT) ACT, 1920 (10 AND 11 GEO. 5, C. 13).

Whereas Section 2, Sub-section (2) of the Profiteering (Amendment) Act, 1920 (10 & 11 Geo. 5, c. 13) provides that the Board of Trade may by Order extend Section 1 of the Profiteering Act, 1919 (9 & 10 Geo. 5, c. 66) to any process of manufacture or to the repairing, altering, dyeing, cleaning, washing, or otherwise treating of any articles mentioned in the Order and processes incidental thereto, subject to such modification as may be necessary to adapt the provisions of that section thereto:

Now, therefore, the Board of Trade do hereby extend Section 1 of the Profiteering Act, 1919 (9 & 10 Geo. 5, c. 66) to the repairing, altering or washing of all articles of wearing apparel (except boots and shoes) and of cloths and dusters, table and bed linen, blankets, towels, mattresses, pillows, bolsters and curtains, and to any processes incidental thereto; to the repairing, altering or cleaning of clocks and watches and to the repairing, or altering of boots, shoes and umbrellas subject to the following modifications, namely: that the words "sale," "seller," and "price" shall include treating or offering to treat in any of the manners aforesaid, any person so doing, and the charge for so doing respectively.

This Order shall come into force as from the ninth day of August, 1920, and may be cited as the Profiteering Acts, 1919 and 1920, Order (No. 9).

Dated this 2nd day of August, 1920.

By the Board of Trade.

R. S. HORNE,
President of the Board of Trade.

STATUTORY RULES AND ORDERS,
1921, No. 203.

OVERSEAS TRADE.

ORDER OF THE BOARD OF TRADE, DATED FEBRUARY 17, 1921, UNDER SECTION 3 OF THE OVERSEAS TRADE (CREDITS AND INSURANCE) ACT, 1920 (10 & 11 GEO. 5, C. 29), ADDING AUSTRIA TO THE SCHEDULE TO THAT ACT.

Whereas by Section 1 of the above-mentioned Act the Board of Trade were empowered to grant credits to persons domiciled in, or to companies incorporated by or under the laws of, the United Kingdom in connection with the export to any country specified in the Schedule to the said Act of goods wholly or partly produced or manufactured in the United Kingdom, subject to the limitations and provisions contained in the said section, and to undertake the business of the insurance of any such goods as aforesaid as therein mentioned.

And whereas by Section 3 of the said Act the Board of Trade were further empowered to add to the said Schedule the name of any country the industrial and financial condition of which has been disorganised by the War.

Now, therefore, in pursuance of the powers in them vested by the above-recited provision and of every other power thereunto them enabling the Board of Trade do hereby order that the country of Austria be added to the Schedule to the said Act.

Dated this 17th day of February, 1921.

R. S. HORNE,
President of the Board of Trade.

STATUTORY RULES AND ORDERS, 1921, No. 363.

TIME.

Summer Time.

ORDER IN COUNCIL DECLARING THE SUMMER TIME ACT, 1916 (6 & 7 GEO. 5, C. 14), AS AMENDED, TO BE IN FORCE DURING THE YEAR 1921.

At the Court at Buckingham Palace, the 9th day of March, 1921.

PRESENT,

The King's Most Excellent Majesty in Council.

Whereas by the Summer Time Act, 1916, as amended by the Time (Ireland) Act, 1916[1], and by the War Emergency Laws (Continuance) Act, 1920[2], it is provided that during the prescribed period in each year in which the first-named Act is in force the time for general purposes is to be one hour in advance of Greenwich Mean Time; and it is further provided that His Majesty may, in any year subsequent to the year 1916, by Order in Council, made during the continuance of the present War and a period of twelve months after the termination thereof, declare the said Act to be in force during that year, and in such case the prescribed period for that year shall be such period as may be fixed by Order in Council:

Now, therefore, His Majesty is pleased, by and with the advice of His Privy Council, to declare, and it is hereby declared, that the Summer Time Act, 1916, as so amended as aforesaid, shall be in force during the year 1921, and the prescribed period in that year shall be from two o'clock in the morning Greenwich Mean Time on Sunday, the 3rd day of April, until two o'clock in the morning Greenwich Mean Time on Monday, the 3rd day of October.

ALMERIC FITZROY.

[1] 6-7 G. 5, c. 45.   [2] 10-1 G. 5, c. 5.

STATUTORY RULES AND ORDERS,

1921, No. $\frac{705}{\text{S. } 34}$.

EMERGENCY.

Explosive Substances.

THE EXPLOSIVE SUBSTANCES (SCOTLAND) ORDER, 1921, DATED APRIL 21, 1921, MADE BY THE SECRETARY FOR SCOTLAND UNDER REGULATION 17 OF THE EMERGENCY REGULATIONS, 1921, WHICH WERE ISSUED UNDER THE EMERGENCY POWERS ACT, 1920 (10 & 11 GEO. 5, C. 55).

In pursuance of the powers conferred on me by Regulation 17 of the Emergency Regulations, 1921[1], I hereby order as follows:

1. A person having in his possession any explosive substance shall keep the same in a secure place approved by the Chief Constable, and shall, if so required by the Chief Constable, remove all or any part of such explosive substance to any place specified by such Chief Constable.

2. This Order shall apply to the Counties of Ayr, Clackmannan, Dumfries, Dumbarton, Fife, Haddington, Kinross, Lanark (including the County of the City of Glasgow), Linlithgow, Midlothian (including the County of the City of Edinburgh), Renfrew and Stirling.

3. This Order may be cited as the Explosive Substances (Scotland) Order, 1921.

ROBERT MUNRO,

(L.S.) His Majesty's Secretary for Scotland.

SCOTTISH OFFICE,
WHITEHALL, LONDON,
21st April, 1921.

[1] S.R. & O., 1921, No. 440.

INDEX OF STATUTES CITED

INDEX OF CASES CITED

GENERAL INDEX

Printed in the United States
By Bookmasters